Cambridge Elements ≡

Elements in Business Strategy
edited by
J.-C. Spender
Kozminski University

STRATEGIZING
IN THE POLISH FURNITURE
INDUSTRY

Paulina Bednarz-Łuczewska
IDEAS Lab, University of Warsaw

CAMBRIDGE
UNIVERSITY PRESS

Shaftesbury Road, Cambridge CB2 8EA, United Kingdom

One Liberty Plaza, 20th Floor, New York, NY 10006, USA

477 Williamstown Road, Port Melbourne, VIC 3207, Australia

314–321, 3rd Floor, Plot 3, Splendor Forum, Jasola District Centre, New Delhi – 110025, India

103 Penang Road, #05–06/07, Visioncrest Commercial, Singapore 238467

Cambridge University Press is part of Cambridge University Press & Assessment, a department of the University of Cambridge.

We share the University's mission to contribute to society through the pursuit of education, learning and research at the highest international levels of excellence.

www.cambridge.org
Information on this title: www.cambridge.org/9781009479400

DOI: 10.1017/9781009091763

First published 2024

A catalogue record for this publication is available from the British Library.

ISBN 978-1-009-47940-0 Hardback
ISBN 978-1-009-09546-4 Paperback
ISSN 2515-0693 (online)
ISSN 2515-0685 (print)

Strategizing in the Polish Furniture Industry

Elements in Business Strategy

DOI: 10.1017/9781009091763
First published online: March 2024

Paulina Bednarz-Łuczewska
IDEAS Lab, University of Warsaw

Author for correspondence: Paulina Bednarz-Łuczewska,
p.luczewska@gmail.com

Abstract: The Element provides a broad overview of the Polish furniture industry. It tells the story of a sector that grew from a bundle of craftsmen into Europe's largest and the world's second-largest furniture exporter within three decades. This is also the story of a sector marked by a subordinate role in global value chains and a mediocre ranking in the global value capture game. Equipped with the methods of anthropology and the theoretical lenses of strategic management, the author guides the reader through the living world of the sector's strategists – their environment, resources, and dilemmas. The Element reconstructs how the strategists engage in creative dialogue with factors at the macro level (semi-peripheral economy, global value chain position), meso level (human capital, governmental programs) and micro level (family traditions, personal interests) to create their unique business models.

This Element also has a video abstract: www.cambridge.org/Paulina

Keywords: furniture industry, strategy, business models, semi-peripheral economy, value chain management

ISBNs: 9781009479400 (HB), 9781009095464 (PB), 9781009091763 (OC)
ISSNs: 2515-0693 (online), 2515-0685 (print)

Contents

1 Introduction   1

2 History   4

3 The Sector and Its Ecosystem   11

4 The Business Models and Value Drivers   30

5 Case Studies   40

6 Conclusions   61

References   63

1 Introduction

There are many reasons why the story of the Polish furniture industry is worth telling.[1] The centuries-long saga has been full of twists and turns and is material for a thriller. The reader with an interest in business strategy may particularly enjoy the polarities that the industry is woven from: grand successes and grand failures, a strong sense of locality yet an intensive global presence, some very unique and some very ordinary elements.

The story of the Polish furniture industry is certainly one of success. By 2022, a sector that had comprised a bundle of craftsmen and some fusty state-owned factories in 1989 had grown into Europe's largest and the world's second largest furniture exporter (surpassed only by China).[2] Furniture production contributes over 2% to the Polish GDP. Polish furniture can be found on every continent: in private homes, top-floor offices, penthouses, schools, hospitals, malls, stadiums and luxury boutiques. The global giant IKEA claims that half of its own production and 20% of its global purchases come from Poland (Inter IKEA Systems B. V., 2021).

The story of the furniture industry in Poland is also one of failure. Some say the industry is wedged between powerful buyers and powerful suppliers. Recently, another pressing force has appeared – human capital shortages. Production and export volumes are high, but margins are shrinking dangerously. According to the much-quoted saying of Piotr Voelkel, the founder of Vox group, Polish furniture production is "blood, sweat and tears" and there is nothing Polish about most furniture produced in the country, except for "toil and wood chips."[3] Indeed, the vast majority of the industry's producers function as low-margin, labor-intensive subcontractors to the international giants. There are only a few Polish brands with international recognition.

Another polarity shaping the Polish furniture industry is the tension between the local and the global. The vast majority of the over 30,000 Polish furniture companies are family firms or firms that started as such. One can still see the impact of craft and local traditions one the culture and practice of the industry. On the other hand, even small firms remain integrated into transnational value chains and experience pressure from international competitors, suppliers and buyers. Moreover, some of the firms have become large global giants, sometimes acquiring or merging with old international players, as is the case of the Nowy Styl Group of Black Red White company.

---

[1] This Element is based on the results of research project nr 2014/15/D/HS4/01173 financed by the National Science Centre in Poland.

[2] B+R Studio, 2022.

[3] https://biznes.gazetaprawna.pl/artykuly/884669,zalozyciel-grupy-vox-meble-bardziej-kocham-syna-niz-firme.html.

Yet another interesting contrast exists between the entrepreneurs that simply try to follow the current and come up with as generic a strategy as possible, and the outliers, whose ingenuity and creativity inspire. One can understand the historic, economic and social forces that have locked many firms into a framework of semi-peripheral, postcolonial capitalism: as cogs in a machine without much agency, they are only able to compete with the low prices (and low margins) achieved through generic means – the availability of wood and a cheap workforce. On the other hand, the reader may be surprised to find out how some strategists have used their imaginative powers to navigate their firms out of this deterministic cage and make them uniquely successful enterprises, which keep exploring new territories.

1.1 Theoretical Framework

To describe is to theorize – every description of a complex reality is based on a set of theoretical assumptions, no matter whether they are articulated or tacit. These assumptions manifest in the various ways an author chooses to mention or omit some facts, to categorize and interpret them. This Element is no exception – it stems from various convictions concerning the nature of strategizing. Let us bring some of them to our attention.

Foremost, we draw from various currents of thought that have placed entrepreneurs and managers at the center of scrutiny as the first principle and origin of any strategy (Sarasvathy, 2001; Spender, 2014; Whittington, 1996; cf. Powell, 2014). Strategizing is presumed to be a profoundly human activity, one that ultimately cannot be contained in a rigorous model, because it is dramatic and open-ended. Such an approach entails much attention paid to case studies that convey unique, phronetic knowledge created within a given context (Flyvbjerg, 2006).

We assume that the strategist operates in a world marked by uncertainty in the classical meaning of the term provided by Frank Knight (1921), that is, the universal epistemological phenomenon, indicating that nobody really knows the possible outcome of the actions while they are being undertaken. But this very uncertainty is responsible for the possibility of value creation (Spender, 2014). The entrepreneurs reach into the unknown with their imagination and engage in action within the concrete space they occupy.

Hence, we do not look at the Polish furniture industry as a set of random data, or as an execution of some eternal laws of economics, while there is a great deal of randomness taking place and one may recognize patterns and developmental trajectories known from other industries. Instead, we view the entire ecosystem as a context in which managerial judgement takes place. We try to reconstruct this context using, as much as possible, the natural language of the industry participants, that is, entrepreneurs, consultants, policymakers and scholars. By zooming in and out of the most basic reality of the industry, that is, the firm, we try to provide the reader with the experience of immersion in the native land of the strategists working in the furniture business in one particular country in Central and Eastern Europe: Poland.

The research behind this Element consisted of observation – a key method in anthropology (Ingold, 2017) often applied to adjacent disciplines. The observation process was multidirectional and lasted for about four years. It consisted of reading the industry research reports, documents and magazines that the industry reads, attending the trade fairs, conferences and zoom meetings the industry attends, and talking to those who have been a part of the ecosystem for decades.

As for the scope of the Element, namely, the boundaries between Polish and non-Polish companies, we looked at the rims set up in Poland by a local entrepreneur and operating at least partially in Poland. Therefore, we did not include in our scrutiny the subsidiaries of international furniture producers; in particular, we considered IKEA a part of the context and not a direct object of research. As for furniture production – we followed the definitions provided by the classification systems in Poland (PKWiU 2015: codes starting with 31) and the EU (The Combined Nomenclature: codes starting with 94).

1.2 Element Structure

The first, introductory section is followed by four main parts and concluding remarks. Section 2 provides an outlook on the historical sources of today's challenges, opportunities and problems. We reconstruct the interplay between Polish history and the development trajectory of the local furniture industry. Section 3 is devoted to the description of the current context in which the furniture producers operate. One gets to know the basic facts about the industry, the main markets and the relationship with the suppliers. It is followed by highlights of the most relevant aspects of the environment – the political context, human capital availability and the culture of the industry. In Section 4, various types of business models are discussed and categorized according to their role in the value chains. This is followed by an overview of the main value drivers in the industry. Section 5 contains seven different case studies. It provides a glance at the lived world of the strategists and their business models. In the concluding Section 6, we summarize the major issues presented throughout the Element.

2 History

The story of the Polish furniture industry cannot be told without reference to the stormy history of the Polish nation. Today's success of the branch as well as its failures and shortcomings has their roots in the past. The unique environment for today's strategic orientations was shaped by the political, social and economic rollercoaster of Polish history. Hence, to understand the context of strategic decisions of the industry in the twenty-first century, one has to have an overview of the historical process forming both the context and the mindsets of the strategists and other stakeholders.

2.1 The Roots

Furniture manufacture has a long tradition in Poland. Rich in ancient forests, manpower and trade routes, the region was destined to excel in carpentry. The earliest accounts of reputable furniture workshops in Niepołomice (near Krakow, then the royal capital) come from the sixteenth century (Kalupa, 2004). This was the time when the Kingdom of Poland was in its best shape, both politically and economically.

Furniture production flourished throughout the seventeenth and eighteenth centuries in various parts of the country despite the gradual decay of the kingdom. Skillfully ornamented furniture pieces made in clusters such as Warsaw or Swarzędz were to be seen in palaces, churches and rich mansions. This was an era when many Polish carpentry hubs developed their own unique, organization style. Craftsmen from Gdansk, for example, were famous for their wardrobes and chairs. Similarly, the small town of Kolbuszowa became known for their exquisitely ornamented furniture, later celebrated as a signature product for the whole region (Maszkowska, 1956). Beside the centers that advanced their original style, there were others that specialized instead in copying the models from Paris or the Netherlands (Pachelska, 2003).

2.1.1 Living under a Glass Ceiling

As the political power of Poland shrank, so did its cultural influence. By 1795 the Polish-Lithuanian Commonwealth was partitioned by the three neighboring empires: Russia, Prussia and Austria. Consequently, economic and technological growth was significantly hindered on the occupied territories. The authorities of the three empires – however liberal – actively served their own bourgeoisie, often through political interventions in the economy and in timber harvesting (Kula, 1947; Pachelska, 2003). Oftentimes business activity on the annexed Polish territories faced unfair competition.

Against all odds, however, furniture was still being produced in the formerly Polish territories and some local workshops were turned into technologically advanced factories. The richness of timber resources kept the production going, even when the region ceased to be famous for its artistry or path-breaking design. The economic situation was fluid, and better times would appear from time to time. In the last two decades of the nineteenth centuries, for example, the pace of growth in the territories controlled by Prussia and Russia was so rapid that the timber industry almost caught up with the rest of Europe (Pachelska, 2003). The exception was southern Poland, annexed by the Austrian Empire. While the rest of the country was growing, the south experienced gradual economic decline resulting in technological backwardness, poverty and social unrest.

2.1.2 Steam-Bent Furniture

Around that time world carpentry was changed by the expansion of the new technology of steam-bent beechwood. It was the invention of a talented Prussian entrepreneur – Michael Thonet, who managed to patent his products and find a mighty protector in the Austrian prince Klemens von Metternich – soon to be one of the most influential politicians of the era (Hoffmanová, 1989). Thanks to the combination of talent and power as well as aggressive marketing, the company Thonet Brothers (Gebrüder Thonet) grew exponentially and became a flagship example of the modern industrial enterprise (Kyriazidou & Pesendorfer, 1999). Light and elegant bentwood chairs, especially the widely acclaimed "Number 14" model designed in 1859, became bestsellers to be seen in almost every respectful Viennese cafe or private house. Over the years, seven factories of the Thonet Brothers were established across Germany and Eastern Europe, including the partitioned territories of Poland. One of the oldest factories established by Thonet Brothers in 1891 in Radomsko, central Poland, still exists nowadays under the name FAMEG. The bentwood patent was limited to a certain territory, so the technology was soon copied by other European furniture producers.

The oldest Polish factory producing bentwood furniture was established in 1870 by the wealthy nobleman Count Leopold Poletyło. This nobleman with a liberal worldview transformed one of his large farms in Wojciechów (in eastern Poland, occupied by Russia in the nineteenth century) into a furniture factory. The enterprise soon became a prosperous joint-stock company co-owned by the local gentry and prominent members of the intelligentsia. The location was very fortunate due to the availability of beechwood and the relative proximity of both Warsaw and the routes to the large centers of the Russian empire – Moscow and Odessa. The company grew rapidly by establishing and acquiring new factories and exporting not only to Russia, but also to France, Holland, Germany as well as to Africa and both Americas. This unprecedented success was made possible by constant innovations in the product realm as well as in human resources management. The company existed until the German attack on Poland in 1939 (Pachelska, 2003).

2.2 Wyspiański and the Tradition of Artistic Design

The trend of the organization of the furniture trade triggered certain resistance in Poland. Various artists of the era turned their attention to the goods of everyday use and explored that realm artistically. Stanislaw Wyspiański, a versatile artist born in Krakow and educated in European cultural centers (Italy, Germany, Switzerland and France) undertook such exploration. The scope of Wyspiański's artistic interests was unbelievably broad – he was an accomplished playwright, but also a versatile visual artist skilled in the techniques of drawing, painting and sculpture. Wyspiański created widely acclaimed theatre scenographies, giant stained-glass windows for medieval churches, not to mention an inspiring, yet controversial, vision of the reconstruction of Wawel Hill – the historic seat of the Polish kings (Gaweł, 2007). Eventually, he harnessed his talent for interior design.

A true artist and bohemian, Wyspiański was disgusted with the idea of mass-produced furniture. He was commissioned to design the interiors of private houses as well as spaces of public use. Indeed, most of his projects were exemplary "Gesamtkunstwerke," total artworks, where every detail from the color of the curtain to a piece of furniture was meticulously selected. Wyspiański's furniture was famously beautiful and notoriously uncomfortable (Kostrzyńska-Miłosz, 2019). According to an anecdote, when asked about the lack of comfort of the chairs he designed for the conference room in the house of the Medical Association, Wyspiański replied that at least the doctors would not fall asleep at the meetings (Żeleński, 1973: 70).

Stanislaw Wyspiański was a truly prominent and inspiring figure. A student and later a professor of the Krakow Academy of Fine Arts, he influenced the way the next generation would view interior design. Typical features of his mindset included organization of the visual and artistic aspects of the piece over its ergonomics and utility as well as disregard for industrial production. For decades to come, the concept of the role of the artist would resonate with generations of designers educated at the fine-art universities throughout Poland. A different, much more user-oriented approach to furniture design would spread later, especially in the end of the twentieth century, with the expansion of capitalism.

2.3 Rising from the Ashes (to Die Again)

World War I (1914–1918) contributed to the almost complete dismantling of economy on the ethnically Polish territories Immersed in battle, the three empires lost any remaining scruples regarding their exploitation of their peripheries. Toward the end of the war, the withdrawing Russian army would confiscate entire enterprises, together with their staff, and move them to Russia or – if this was not an option – they would blow up the entire plant (Jezierski & Leszczyńska, 1997). German and Austrian armies destroyed the infrastructure of the abandoned territories: many mines, railways and bridges were blasted to guarantee that the rising country would not pose an economic threat.

On November 11, 1918, the very day that the Great War ended, Poland regained its independence, but the country was in ruins. Partitioned for 126 years, Poland had to rebuild all of her institutions, establish and strengthen her borders, and revive the devastated economy. The three parts of the country formerly occupied by three different empires had different currencies, legal systems and social norms. Cargo transport was difficult because of the damage done to the roads and railways, not to mention the discrepancy between railway systems in the prior Russian partition and the rest of the country (the Russians railways are slightly broader than the European ones). Despite the end of World War I, the Polish army was still involved in military conflict with the Bolsheviks for two more years. Therefore the government maintained many wartime economic regulations, including the strict control of the sales of crucial raw materials (Pachelska, 2003).

For the wood industry, the two years after the war were a time of a deep reset. Value chains were discontinued. Due to wartime perturbations, many sawmills were dismantled, and the timber trade was destabilized because of speculation. The changing conditions caused many companies to disappear. Investors were too afraid to finance new enterprises, so the state had to accept the role of investor as well as economic regulator (Pachelska, 2003).

The following first decade of freedom (1920–1929) brought a considerable improvement in the economic situation of the region. Moderate inflation and favorable worldwide trends as well as deep governmental reforms contributed to steady economic growth. The volume of industrial production gradually reached prewar levels and exceeded them. The entire woodworking industry grew because the boom in construction caused a demand for wooden products, including furniture (Pachelska, 2003). The need to unify the legal system concerning the wood trade as well as the high demand for timber prompted the Polish government to strongly intervene in this branch. The regulations were truly far-reaching, including a ban on timber export without direct permission from the Ministry of Agriculture and State Property, which was in force for two years after the war. Even once the timber supply had stabilized, the state regulated the harvest and trade of wood. This led to repetitive custom work with neighboring Germany, a country of incomparably larger economic and political power.

In 1924 the government established a state-controlled organization called Polish State Forests responsible for the administration of forest areas. Polish State Forests and their policy have been one of the crucial factors shaping the environment for the Polish timber industry ever since. During the 1930s, the organization was further modernized to ensure the rational and sustainable exploitation of timber. In order to enable the commercial activity of the State Forests, in 1931 the Council of Ministers' Economic Committee founded the PAGED Polish Export Agency (Polska Agencja Eksportu), a company seated in the port town of Gdynia. PAGED, formally a subsidiary of the State Forests, took over the entire process of the timber trade – from financial negotiations with clients from the country and from abroad, to storage in the ports and product shipment (Pachelska, 2007).

One cannot speak of a full-fledged Polish furniture industry in the interwar period because industrial production remained at an early stage of development. The most advanced subsector on the path to industrialization was bent wood furniture production, the branch that was born as an industrial technology. In 1937, the 36 bentwood factories on Polish territory employed more people than the 245 factories producing other types of furniture (Kalupa, 2004: 17). Most of the furniture for internal markets was produced by small businesses based on handicraft and simple technology. These small-scale production facilities were often located close to each other, forming aggregations that would one day develop into clusters. Even before World War II, one could observe two main currents of development of furniture manufacturing – industrial production and the handicraft.

The process of growth of the furniture production branch was hindered anew by World War II and the six years of Nazi occupation. Poland again became a battlefield and the subject of ruthless devastation.

Alongside industrial furniture production prone to economic and social shocks as well as artistic furniture design that remained an economically insignificant niche, there existed the traditional craft referred to as "the people's industry." It consisted of small producers of simple wooden products such as barrels, wheelbarrows, spades, kitchen utensils and basic furniture (Pachelska, 2003: 100). This craft was particularly common in southern Poland, formerly occupied by Austria, and it thrived, supported by the still-favorable natural conditions and despite the unfavorable economic and political conditions.

2.4 Communist Times

The decades after World War II were a time of deep economic and social changes in a Europe divided by the Iron Curtain. In the West, birth rates skyrocketed and the strong will to rebuild the destroyed continent resulted in an unprecedented boom in construction and related branches. Economies developed rapidly; the middle class grew bigger and richer. The advertising industry became very influential in shaping popular tastes, including those concerning interior design. Homes became not only places to live in, but also attributes of class identity. Western Europe witnessed the emergence of the modern consumer society.

These processes boosted the growth of the Western European furniture industry. High demand for quality items prompted producers to search for innovation both in production technology and in material engineering. The discovery of new types of glues as well as techniques of wood coloring created more space for design in furniture production. This was also the time when various wood-based panels ware introduced to industrial furniture production on a mass scale – the material was cheaper, more malleable and easier to transport. New trends in design popularized artificial and natural veneers on furniture surfaces. In other words, the market for mass-produced furniture was vast and the industry flourished.

The situation in Eastern Europe was different. The first postwar reactions of the population were akin to their western neighbors – they wanted to settle down, have babies and rebuild their countries. Yet Soviet restrictions prevented the Eastern bloc, including Poland, from accepting financial assistance and economic knowledge transfers from the United States (the so-called Marshall Plan). Fully subdued to the political plans of the communists, the economy did not take advantage of the positive trends and hence its growth was considerably hindered in comparison to their counterparts from the West.

In Poland, the trajectory of development of industrial production of furniture and craft-based carpentry bifurcated at this point. After the war, industrial enterprises were nationalized by the Polish communist state. This opened some export possibilities for them within the post-Soviet bloc, but the system of politicized and centrally controlled economy turned out to be uncompetitive; hence, no state enterprise could truly thrive. The Soviet authorities would practice sheer exploitation of the controlled territories, sometimes outside of any legal boundaries.

Polish forests were exploited ruthlessly. "Neighborly trade" was the euphemism for predatory practices. The monopolistic Foreign Trade Centers would buy various products in Polish sawmills and furniture factories and sell them for a fraction of the value to Russian plants, which would resell them as their own production. The managers of the Foreign Trade Centers knew that "neighborly trade" was high priority and had to be performed timely and with due diligence.[4]

The trade, however, was left on its own while it had to struggle against the privileged position of the state-owned businesses on every step of the value chain. The simple workshops producing furniture for local needs preserved the spirit of traditional woodworking. There was no place for a sophisticated strategy – hard work combined with stamina and quick-wittedness in overcoming the obstacles. The dominant mindset that emerged from this kind of life included the belief in strong familial and local ties, resistance to change and distrust political discourse.

The nationalized industrial producers of furniture were better off during communist times as they were in perfect "synch" with the centrally controlled economy. In the 1950s, the government undertook several actions to cluster the scattered single-factory units under common umbrella organizations. These larger entities were able to export to the West and earn the Western currencies that the communist regimes so craved. Over the next decades, the authorities invested heavily in the furniture industry, making it technologically advanced and up-to-date with contemporary design trends.

This led to collaborations with companies worldwide, including ones outside the Eastern bloc. One such encounter changed the course of the entire branch for decades. In 1961, a promising entrepreneur from Sweden named Ingmar Kampran, the founder and president of IKEA, came to the town of Radomsko to order the manufacture of 500 Ögla chairs made of bent wood. The FAMEG company where this memorable order was placed had evolved out of a factory established in 1881 by the Thonet Brothers. Kampran, who had troubled relations with the furniture branch in his homeland, quickly tightened his collaboration with Polish producers, bringing their Western capital and know-how to Poland.

2.5 The Game Changer – 1989 and After

The real game changer came in December 1988 as the declining Polish communist government introduced a new law that lifted the ban on private economic activity. Most of today's Polish furniture giants started as small workshops founded around that time.

The 1990s brought a short golden era: the sudden opening of a super-absorbent post-Soviet market. Within the window of a few years, some companies grew by twenty, fifty or several hundred times.

---

[4] Information from the eyewitness, Mieczysław Lewicki.

The tide changed suddenly. In 1998 Russia imposed a very high duty on imported goods. Any export to Russia became pointless. A number of Polish furniture producers lost their main market almost overnight. The domestic market wasn't even remotely large enough to absorb the extra supply.

The closing of their lucrative eastern market forced the already large factories to look west and south in search of new markets. The German market turned out to be very different from the Russian one, however, demanding quality, timeliness and organization – every newcomer had to adjust to the rules of the game set up by the local giants a long time ago. This forced quick learning on the side of many young and ambitious entrepreneurs. It was this pivotal moment when most of today's largest Polish furniture companies were established.

The general enthusiasm for business activity, the availability of a cheap workforce and strong local and familial ties created conditions where Polish furniture entrepreneurs overcame most of their shortcomings. Their businesses survived and thrived. By the end of the decade, a few Polish furniture companies put up modest exhibition stands at the most prestigious European fairs in Milan and Cologne and thus entered the big world. Within three decades, the Polish furniture industry had reached the shape presented further in this Element.

3 The Sector and Its Ecosystem

3.1 Basic Statistics

For several years, Poland has been one of the leading producers and exporters of furniture in the world (Figure 2). There are only a few other economic sectors where Polish production is equally successful. In 2020, Poland was the second largest exporter and the sixth larger producer of furniture in the world. The ranking of the largest furniture manufacturers in the world in 2020 is opened by China, with a value of furniture production of approximately USD 170 billion. The runner-up is the United States, with USD 56.3 billion. The next places belong to European countries: Germany and Italy, ahead of India and Poland. In 2020, Poland produced furniture worth USD 13.6 billion. The next three places in the ranking are occupied by Asian countries, namely, Vietnam, South Korea and Japan (Figure 1). Canada with USD 8.6 closes the TOP 10 ranking (B+R STUDIO Tomasz Wiktorski, 2022).

Vietnam has been able to take advantage of the trade war between the United States and China and take over some portion of the American market, and Vietnamese producers increased the value of furniture production from USD 4.4 billion in 2008 to USD 11.8 billion in 2020. With such a dynamic, Poland may soon be outrun as a producer and exporter by Vietnam.

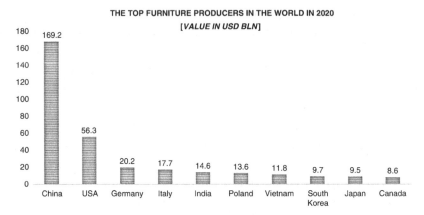

Figure 1 The top furniture producers in the world, 2020 (B+R STUDIO Tomasz Wiktorski, 2022).

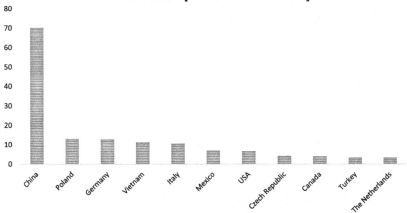

Figure 2 The top furniture exporters in the world, 2020 (B+R STUDIO Tomasz Wiktorski, 2022).

Among the leading furniture manufacturers, Poland – before Canada and Italy – had the highest value of furniture production per million inhabitants in the world, which in 2020 amounted to USD 359 million (B+R STUDIO Tomasz Wiktorski, 2022).

The furniture industry remains one of the sectors crucial to the Polish economy. In the years 2014–2021 furniture production contributed over 2% to the Polish GDP. The branch employs about 200,000 people (B+R STUDIO Tomasz Wiktorski, 2022). The Polish furniture sector ranks second in Europe (after Italy) in terms of registered furniture companies. In 2021, there were over 32,000 such companies in Poland. Out of these, 81 were large companies with more than 250 employees, 291 medium-sized companies (50–249 employees), 1 232 small companies (10–49 employees) and over 30,000 microenterprises with less than 10 employees (B+R STUDIO Tomasz Wiktorski, 2022) comprise the industry. In 2020, large and medium-sized firms were responsible for 74.6% of the value of sold furniture production in Poland; the 30,000 microenterprises realized 7.9% of this value (B+R STUDIO Tomasz Wiktorski, 2022).

Analysts point to various interdependent factors that contribute to the strong position of the furniture industry in Poland. The primary ones are geographical, natural and historic, while the secondary ones stem from the long-standing presence of furniture production in the country. They include:

a) competitive production costs, in particular due to lower labor costs compared to Europe, which translates into a favorable price-quality ratio;

b) a long-standing tradition that results in a high technical culture of production and the presence of the entire ecosystem;

c) relative availability of qualified specialists on the labor market (especially until recently);

d) high production potential and flexibility of some producers who can quickly adapt to the changing needs of customers;

e) relatively abundant natural resources of wood as a key raw material, together with a well-developed local wood-based sector; and

f) an attractive geographic location – close to absorbent markets in Western Europe.

One has to note, however, that for the past couple of years these traditional advantages have been shrinking or losing their pivotal role.

The furniture industry primarily comprises companies with Polish ownership. The large role of domestic capital in a sector that is so heavily export-oriented is not a frequent case in the Polish economy. The share of domestic companies in the total revenues of the furniture industry is approximately 63%, which is one of the highest (Pekao SA, 2021). This feature makes furniture manufacturing a branch of particular interest among policy makers.

Furniture production in Poland is highly geographically concentrated. The three regions with the largest share of furniture manufacturing – Wielkopolskie, Zachodniopomorskie and Warmińsko-Mazurskie – are responsible for more than half of the entire production in the country (Pekao SA, 2021).

The largest Polish furniture manufacturers (according to net revenues in 2020) are presented in Table 1.

Table 1 The 15 largest furniture producers in Poland, ranked by revenue in 2020 (B+R STUDIO Tomasz Wiktorski, 2022).

Rank	Name of the Firm	Revenues in 2020 (EUR) (1 EUR = 4.4459 PLN)	Year to year change (%)
1	IKEA Industry Poland Sp. z o.o.	1 041 751 689	-4. 9
2	Correct Sp.k.	281 557 339,8	-6.3
3	Black Red White S.A.	273 767 910,2	5.2
4	Fabryka Mebli Forte S.A.	247 442 362,6	-2.4
5	Com.40 Sp. z o.o. sp.k.	241 911 571,1	-16.9
6	Steinpol Central Services sp. z o.o.	188 154 437,6	13.1
7	Nowy Styl Sp. z o.o.	171 425 250,5	-8.5
8	Szynaka-Meble Sp. z o.o.	144 981 313,1	-4.8
9	Grupa G-3 Sp.j.	138 005 849,9	-11.8
10	Sits Sp. z o.o.	128 697 513,2	4.1
11	Meble Wójcik Sp. z o.o.	123 427 709,6	2.1
12	DFM Sp. z o.o.	119 314 530,5	16.3
13	Adriana S.A.	114 902 781,4	4.9
14	Hilding Anders Polska Sp. z o.o.	103 681 881,7	-3.3
15	Fabryka Mebli Bodzio Sp.j.	90 652 750,85	0.6

Financially speaking, the sector is rather healthy. The average profitability from sales from 2017 to 2020 fluctuated between 4.5% in 2018 to 6.7% in 2020 (B+R STUDIO Tomasz Wiktorski, 2022).

In the years 2017–2020 the debt ratio (the ratio of liabilities to assets) was at a stable level of approx. 40%, clearly below the average for the manufacturing as a whole (47–48%). In the same years, the quick liquidity ratio was around 1.1, which is in the range considered to be optimal (Pekao SA, 2021).

One could assume that with a favorable liquidity and debt situation the industry should be engaged in long-term investments. This is, however, not quite the case, and the branch remains conservative in its approach to investments. In the years 2016–2020, the average ratio of investment outlays to industry revenues was approx. 3.7%, and in relation to depreciation, approx. 1.3%. For the entire manufacturing sector, values were 4.4% and 1.4%, respectively (Pekao SA, 2021). This might indicate that industry stakeholders are worried about the future and doubtful about the sustainability of their competitive edge. In 2021, one of the largest domestic producers, the Forte Group, announced they would abandon their plan to build a giant, state-of-the-art production plant that was planned to be finished by 2023.

3.2 Market Segments

The segments of the furniture market can be differentiated based on various criteria:

(a) the types of products (shelves, wardrobes, chairs, tables, sofas, etc.);
(b) the types of raw material used (solid wood, fiberboard, synthetics, glass, textiles and foams, metal, etc.);
(c) the types of the project (repetitive mass production of catalogue products for individual clients as opposed to contracts for custom-made furnishing for institutional clients);
(d) the designated space (workplace furniture, home furniture: bedroom, kitchen, bathroom, etc.); and
(e) the designated market (domestic market, export to EU, non-EU, overseas, etc.).

The choice of a segment in which a given company operates (often it is a mixture) is an important part of the firm's identity and thus of their business model (Spender 2014).

The first two criteria are particularly important because they translate into other fundamental choices, like ones about technological investments and marketing strategy. Companies often specialize in one type of the market, but there are also firms present on various markets.

Every furniture company must situate itself on the value chain and this is yet another fundamental decision, one regarding the type of business model (further described in Section 4). Roughly speaking, the value-added chain includes the stages such as: design, raw material and parts supplies, production, marketing and distribution and sometimes extra service (assembly, maintenance, etc.). The company takes over one (production) or more functions. Each of the stages may bring a portion of profit to a firm, but the distribution of margins along the value chain is not necessarily proportionate or even. Therefore, the key game played by the firms that participate in the value-added process is that of value capture (Bowman & Ambrosini, 2000; Gans & Real, 2017). They all seek ways to gain a bigger portion of the total profit.

3.3 The Domestic Market

Among European countries, Germany and Italy produce more furniture than Poland (measured by value), and yet the former countries export slightly less (as for 2021 and 2022). This is because of their high internal demand. As for Poland, the majority of furniture produced is being exported, because the internal market is still relatively shallow. Its estimated value in 2021 was approximately PLN 10–12 billion (EUR 2–2,5 billion) (Pekao SA, 2021). Considering the thirty-eight million population of the country, this is a relatively small value – for example, the German market is estimated at EUR 20–22 billion, which means about four times higher expenses per capita (Pekao SA, 2021).

The demand for new housing remains high in Poland. The city lifestyle includes a carefully designed apartment, and the generally growing purchasing power and consumer awareness mean that the demand for furniture, including products from the higher price segments, is constantly growing. And yet this growth is too slow to close the gap with Western Europe any time soon, causing the departure of the export-orientation within the industry. In 2019, an average Polish person spent 163.1 EUR on furniture, while the average furniture expenditure per capita in Europe is 295.7 EUR (1009 EUR in Switzerland) (PKO BP, 2021).

When it comes to domestic furniture distribution channels, they vary between various business models. Office furniture is sold mostly on the business-to-business model as a part of a turnkey service of interior design. As far as furniture for individual users are concerned, some producers use their own retail network and some partner up with larger distributors.

Among the interior design stores in Poland, IKEA, Jysk, Agata Meble and the BRW (Black Red White Furniture) group generate the highest turnover. It should be remembered that a significant part of the turnover of furniture stores are widely understood interior design items, and the stores themselves are adapting their business model toward interior design stores (B+R STUDIO Tomasz Wiktorski, 2022).

3.3.1 IKEA (Ingka Group) in Poland

IKEA has played a pivotal role in the development of the furniture industry in Poland. Since their legendary order of the first batch of chairs in 1961 from a furniture manufacturer in Radomsko, IKEA has become the hub around which the industry grew. The multinational retailer gradually built a complex ecosystem of suppliers and subcontractors. In 1991 IKEA opened its own production company – the Swedwood (today IKEA Industry). Apart from that, IKEA would regularly collaborate with several subcontractors. The companies that partnered up with IKEA got a chance to exploit their production capacities and, what is even more important, learn a lot about the quality standards on the Western European markets. Collaboration with IKEA was widely considered to be a voucher for a company's reliability and conscientiousness.

Many of today's top furniture companies have grown as IKEA's subcontractors, among them Com40, Correct, ProfiM, Szynaka Group, or Adriana, to name just a few. For many of them, IKEA is still an important part of their operations. Today IKEA Industry is by far the largest furniture manufacturer in Poland, but the retailer still collaborates with 79 local producers. As the company points out, every third piece of furniture sold worldwide in IKEA stores has been manufactured in Poland.

3.4 Foreign Markets

Poland is the second largest furniture exporter in the world, surpassed only by China. Moreover, export is the major driving force for the Polish furniture sector. The production capacity of the Polish furniture manufacturers exceeds domestic demand by far. In fact, in the recent decade total production was as much as ten times larger than domestic consumption. Polish furniture is sold primarily to the European Union.

The Polish top export item is a sofa with a sleeping function – in fact, in 2020 35% of the world export of this type of furniture came from Poland (Pekao SA, 2021). Other often exported types include: mattresses (13%), upholstered seating furniture (12%), wooden home furniture (10%), furniture parts (7%) and wooden office furniture (7%) (Pekao SA, 2021).

3.4.1 Germany

The German market is crucial for the Polish furniture industry. In the second and third decade of the twentieth century, the German share in the total export value of Polish furniture varied between 34% and 40% (PFR, 2021). Just as was the case with the Russian market in the 1990s, today the existence and prosperity of the large part of the Polish furniture companies depends on the German market. Germany is the most obvious export destination due to its size and geographical proximity (OIGPM, 2021). Therefore, Polish producers make sure to attend the largest German furniture trade fair – ORGATEC (for workplace furniture) and IMM (for home furniture) in Cologne.

The furniture imported from Poland to Germany adds up to about 16% of the total demand (PFR, 2021). Since 2020, the value of import from China per year has exceeded that from Poland. Seating furniture and parts of seating furniture account for 40% of the goods exported (PARP, 2018a).

The major competitors, especially in the higher price segments, are the domestic producers – highly consolidated and experienced. German furniture companies are usually older and have a profound know-how about the distribution system. They gather in strong furniture associations (e.g. Begros, GfM Trend, Garant, EMV, Alliance, Union) which have enough power to influence distributors and producers through pricing policy and specific requirements. Moreover, it is extremely difficult to promote a new brand name on the German market, whereas the old, local brands have gained their visibility over many years. It is a typical practice that the end user only learns about the brand-name of the distributor and not that of the producer. Polish producers often say that it is "almost impossible" to promote their own brand among the end-users. This translates to lower profitability.

In comparison to other European markets, the German market is very structured. Distribution is dominated by large, omnipotent purchasing groups. That is why the market is less available for SMEs with a minimum bargaining power. The typical business model on this market is either an agreement with a large distributor (a retailer, a purchasing group, etc.) or the role of a subcontractor responsible only for the manufacturing of an item designed and sold by another company and under their brand name. The dominant competitive advantage of the Polish producers is price.

The German market is also believed to be very demanding. German clients have high expectations concerning the quality of both products and the services attached. That is why it was not an easy transition for many Polish companies to export to Germany instead of Russia, when the latter market closed in 1998. For many Polish furniture companies the reorientation required a deep change in their business model. This is why a strong presence on the German market is a token of success. Cases of Polish companies having acquired old German companies (e.g. Nowy Styl or Szynaka) inspire admiration and are widely commented by other Polish producers, usually with satisfaction akin to the joy of football fans celebrating their team's victory.

3.4.2 The Czech Republic

The second biggest recipient of Polish furniture is the Czech Republic. The market is small, but Poland has a large share in it (about 30% in 2020) (PFR, 2021). The Czech Republic has a strong domestic production sector, but over the last three decades, furniture from Poland has exerted pressure on it to a large extent. The Polish product is slightly cheaper – a factor of crucial importance in the low-price market segment. The dominant product type is non-wooden parts for seating furniture (about 70% of the export volume). In other words, in the dominant business model, the Polish producers of furniture parts are subcontractors of the local companies that take over the rest (more lucrative) part of the value chain. It is hard to say if this model will be sustainable in the long run. The most important Czech furniture fair is called Mobitech and it is organized annually in Brno.

3.4.3 Great Britain

Despite Brexit, Great Britain remains an important destination for Polish furniture exporters. In 2020, 7.4% of the furniture imported came from Poland, making the country the third largest recipient of Polish furniture (Pekao SA, 2021). The market is vast with much larger middle- and upper-price segments as compared to the Czech one. In 2019, 11% of furniture revenues in the UK were generated by online stores, which is slightly above the world's average. The dominant product types are seating furniture parts and upholstered seating furniture (sofas, armchairs, etc.) (PFR, 2021).

3.4.4 Non-European Markets

Generally speaking, the EU market expects Polish furniture to be solid but affordable. It is difficult to crack the glass ceiling of the economic segment. With rising production costs in Poland and the pressing price competition from Asia, the industry seeks other prospective markets where they could build a fresh identity and compete by virtues other than low price. Three markets stick out despite the geographical distance: Kazakhstan, the Middle East (UAE, Saudi Arabia and Qatar) and the United States.

Along with the individual promotion of various firms (showrooms, fairs, etc.) there were some collective marketing actions aiming at promotion of the Polish furniture brands in these places. These common actions are in most cases co-sponsored by various governmental agencies.

In 2017, the Polish Chamber of Commerce of Furniture Manufacturers in collaboration with the governmental agencies launched a program promoting Polish furniture during the EXPO in the Kazakh capital of Astana (today Nur-Sultan). The Kazakh furniture market is growing fast and presence there might open a gateway to various other Asian destinations. With the Russian attack on Ukraine the situation has become more problematic, since Kazakhstan might easily become a Russian ally and thus exclude itself from trade relations with Poland.

Another prospective destination is the Middle East. The market is absorbent and dynamic, but also very demanding. The contract market might be particularly lucrative; however, expectations concerning quality of the product and also overall customer experience are very high. The Chamber of Commerce and the administration promoted Polish furniture producers and brands during the two important events in Dubai – EXPO 2020 and Index Dubai 2019 – the largest furniture and interior design fair in the Middle East and North Africa regions. It is difficult to tell if these attempts were successful. So far, the Middle East remains a marginal export destination.

The American furniture market is the largest in the world. In 2019, the value of furniture sold accounted for EUR 230 billion, leaving the runner-up India far behind (EUR 171.8 billion). In 2020, seven Polish furniture brands (Benix, Black Red White, Gala Collezione, Raw, Szynaka Meble, Vzór and Zieta Studio) were presented in a showroom during the largest furniture fair in the United States, in High Point, North Carolina. The project was a joint initiative of the Polish Chamber of Commerce of Furniture Manufacturers and the Polish National Foundation. The expectations of American clients and retailers differ from the European ones, and the Polish producer still needs to get to know them. The costs of transatlantic shipment are high, so the economic segment can hardly be a target for Polish producers. Nevertheless, with a proper export scale, the United States might become a profitable new market for Polish producers.

3.5 The Supplies

The COVID-19 pandemic and the Russian invasion of Ukraine severely destabilized the supply chains and prices of all the basic materials used in furniture production, such as wood (solid and wood-based panels), textiles, upholstery foams and metal elements. In 2022 the cost of raw materials became one of the crucial factors shaping the profitability of the industry.

3.5.1 Wood

The basic material in furniture production is wood in different forms: wood-based panels of different sorts (e.g. chipboards, medium-density fiberboards, beaverboard), plywood, solid wood, wooden veneer and others.

One of the strategic advantages of the timber industry in Poland has been the proximity of vast state-owned forest areas. The relation between the timber industry and the governmental agency State Forests (Lasy Państwowe) has always been tense, as the interests of the two often diverge. The agency aims to export timber in order to get better bargains from the foreign buyers. Sometimes it also limits the supply to make sure that the tillage is sustainable and the resources will be renewed. The industry, in turn, would like to limit the export and make the supply more flexible, to follow the demand for wooden products. However, domestic forests are not the only source of wood for the furniture production. Forty percent of neighboring Belarus is covered with forests, and the timber industry is one of the key branches in the country. Additionally, Ukraine and Russia used to be important sources of wood import.

The COVID-19 pandemic already destabilized the wood supply and the price of timber rose significantly – from 200% to 600% – everywhere in the world. The Russian invasion of Ukraine in 2022 and the ensuing ban on timber import from Belarus and Russia have made the situation even more difficult. The import from Belarus alone used to satisfy 27% of the Polish demand. The representatives of timber industries entered into a dispute with State Forests insisting that the agency should increase the supply of wood domestically by putting limits on timber export, especially to non-EU countries, and by fulfilling the obligations of the agreement already signed. They even petitioned the Ministry of Development and Technology to side with the industry in the conflict. Difficult times exacerbate conflicts that would otherwise be resolved peacefully.

3.5.2 Wood-Based Panels

The market of the wood-based panels in Central and Eastern Europe is dominated by a handful of strong players: Egger, Kronospan, Swiss Krono and Pfleiderer. These are multinational corporations operating all over the world. Their bargaining power has been high for years, and it may become even higher. In 2022 Kronospan announced its plan to acquire Pfleiderer Polska, the Polish subsidiary of the German giant. The European Commission initiated an investigation to assess the planned acquisition. The Commission is concerned that the merger may restrict competition in the supply of different types of wood-based panels in Poland and neighboring regions.

One case may shed some light on the situation. In 2015 one of the biggest Polish companies listed on the Warsaw stock exchange – Capital Group Forte – decided to build two very modern production plants. One plant was supposed to produce wood-based panels and ensure a stable supply for the Group. The second was supposed to be a furniture production plant with a production line designed by Homag, one of the world leaders in the machine making industry. The Forte Group bragged that the facility would be one of the largest and most advanced in Europe. The wood-based panel production site was built and launched in 2018 and cost almost EUR 130 million, of which 10 million was covered by a state subsidy. Yet the construction of the furniture factory has been canceled. Due to this cancellation, the Forte Group was not able to fulfil one of the conditions from the subsidy agreement, namely the creation of 910 work-places. The company justified the change of plans with force majeure, that is, the outbreak of the COVID-19 pandemic and its impact on the increase in raw material prices, as well as a decline in market demand and uncertainty about demand in the near future. The explanation wasn't accepted by the Ministry of Development and Technology, and the company has to return the subsidy with interest.

3.5.3 Other Raw Materials

Other materials for furniture production include upholstery foams, textiles, laminates and various metal elements. Less common are plastic elements and glass. Wood-based panels, plywood and sometimes also furniture production require synthetic rosins and other chemical binders. The cost of production is also determined by energy prices. Of the aforementioned commodities, uphol-stery foam requires a special focus. The large part of the furniture exported from Poland belongs to the category of "seating furniture," that is, a commodity type that often requires the use of foam. The foams are mostly imported form Asia. The disruption in the supply chains caused by the pandemic as well as the rise in energy and fuel prices has contributed to the sudden increase of the foam prices. The industry is unable to make a quick turnaround and acquire the foam elsewhere, so the additional cost has to be dealt with.

3.5.4 Machinery

The furniture making industry requires machinery – from a basic machine set to the complex park prepared for the fourth industrial revolution. There are many producers of machines, and the price range is very broad. Among the most renowned producers one can name Anthon, Biesse Group, Homag, ICA Group, Intec, IMA Klessmann, SCM Group, Weima or Weinig. The Polish furniture producers often mention Homag as a synonym of quality. Many of the leading producers originate in Germany, but the competition from Asia is also quite strong. There are some local machinery producers, such as Allcomp – a very successful producer of machines used in upholstered furniture production.

Furniture is usually transported in parcels containing parts that can be easily assembled at their destination. The drilling process for such furniture must be very precise to make sure that the assembly process will be smooth and easy. The most common furniture fittings are standardized, so there are only few possible ways of attaching them. Large drilling machines are programmed to make the holes that correspond with a chosen type of fitting. Such machines, however, are large and expensive.

This led to an interesting innovation developed by a Polish inventor and entrepreneur – Krzysztof Brzeziński. He invented a hand drill able to operate in a very precise way, thanks to a set of rudimentary tools and some Newtonian physics. The ISKRA drill won several awards at various fairs and exhibitions and now it is sold to microfirms, making them able to ship their products in parcels and thus broadening the portfolio of clients and products. The drill is very affordable; the price is similar to that of a regular hand drill.

3.5.5 The Struggle for Value Capture

As has been demonstrated earlier, the pandemic and then the war in Ukraine caused a sudden increase in the raw material prices but also in the costs of energy and logistics. The crisis destabilized the relationship between the various links of the value chain. Each player wants to keep the same level of profitability; no one wants to be burdened with the additional cost.

With the pressing price competition from China, the industry is not powerful enough to shift the additional cost to its end users. While the customer price can be raised, clients will not accept a change of price that would ensure the same level of profitability. Therefore, the whole value chain has entered a state of struggling for power. The "weaker player" is expected to cushion the shock of decreasing profitability. In the dominant business models for the Polish industry, where the manufacturer is a subcontractor of a larger entity (purchasing group, retailer, a strong brand name holder) the large part of the "cost penalty" is imposed on the manufacturer. Despite the nominally higher revenues, many Polish producers complain that their average profitability has dropped from about 6% to about 4%.

3.6 The Political Context

The furniture industry in Poland has survived various political systems, not to mention various governments, and is not known to be politically biased or active. The business has its own agenda, often independent from the political realm. Yet the sector became big enough to attract the interest of politicians and policymakers. Furniture manufacturing is present in the political narrative of the ruling party as an example of a national success. Since the year 2017, the government has pursued an active policy promoting the industry as a part of a broader plan. In 2017 The Polish government officially adopted the Strategy for Responsible Development (SRD) – the key document for the Polish State in the field of medium- and long-term economic policy.

3.6.1 The Strategy for Responsible Development (SRD)

The Strategy for Responsible Development (SRD)[5] is anything but generic. The document assumes a controversial diagnosis of the Polish neoliberal transformation as well as an applicable list of objectives to be accomplished in the years to come.

The document identifies five main challenges faced by Poland and defines them as "development traps." These are:

Middle income trap. The GDP per capita of Poland is only 45% of GDP per capita in the United States. The relatively fast development of the previous decade was due to European funds, foreign investments, and a cheap labor force. All of these growth levers are gradually expiring. New motors for development must bring productivity growth and competitiveness along with an increase in remunerations. "Wage-led growth" is the most eligible one for the Polish economy.

Imbalance trap. Healthy development requires a balance between foreign and domestic capital. Meanwhile in Poland, the latter is scarce and unstable.

Average product trap. The dominant business model of a Polish exporter is the delivery of non-complex products at the lowest possible price. Only 8% of Polish export is innovation-based. Polish firms are hardly ever world champions. Only 1% of the GDP is spent on R&D.

Demographic trap. Population ageing leads to workforce paucity and places a heavy fiscal burden on the working-age cohorts.

---

[5] www.gov.pl/web/fundusze-regiony/informacje-o-strategii-na-rzecz-odpowiedzialnego-rozwoju visited on February 28, 2022.

Institutional weakness trap. State institutions are inefficient, creating an environment that is unfriendly for local entrepreneurs and ineffective in the pursuit of serious economic offenders.

There are several objectives and corrective actions that the SRD stipulated to redirect the development trajectory of the Polish economy out of the five traps. Some of the projected actions were particularly relevant for the furniture industry.

The main novelty that the SRD document introduced was a focused, selective economic policy. The strategic document identified the branches that have already been successful on the global market and therefore deserve governmental support. Furniture manufacturing was mentioned alongside the automotive, chemical, hardware and food industries. The government promised to actively support their development and competitiveness on the global market via dedicated programs. The expectation was that with the smart support from the state, the domestic firms would expand globally, multiplying the desired Polish capital and providing valuable workplaces.

There were several actions undertaken in the aftermath of the SRD adoption supporting the furniture industry. The most notable were the Polish Furniture Program, Export Accelerator, financing the development of the marketing strategy for the "Polish Furniture" brand as well as the "Go to Brand" program.

3.6.2 The Polish Furniture Flagship Program

Soon after the SRD was adopted, the newly created Polish Development Fund launched the "Polskie Meble" (Polish Furniture) flagship program. Its objectives were:

1. To change the image of the Polish furniture industry and associate it with a high-quality brand.
2. To become the European export leader by 2020.
3. To become the European leader in furniture production (measured by volume) by 2030.

3.6.3 Export Accelerator

The Export Accelerator project was launched in 2018. It was targeted at companies with a majority share of Polish capital and significant production potential which sell original products under their own brand and are ready for foreign expansion. The program was free of charge and consisted of three elements. The first one – New Markets Zone – offered general trainings about the various pro-export tools that the Fund could offer, as well as access to the international network of Polish foreign trade offices and dedicated industry events. The second element – Companies' Zone – consisted of customized consulting by the fund's experts as well as various forms of financial aid. The third one – Dialog Zone – was particularly innovative. It offered fast-track access to public administration officials and experts in order to respond to the emerging legal and administrative constraints. The Accelerator was generally well accepted by the industry; the most important branch organization, the Polish Chamber of Commerce of Furniture Manufacturers has granted its patronage over the program.[6]

3.6.4. The Polish Furniture Brand

The concept of an umbrella brand of Polish furniture was given a lot of attention. The governmental agency commissioned an in-depth analysis of the issue published in a form of ten state-of-the art research reports. The researchers analyzed the potential of the brand, the trends on the market as well as other national brand images (PARP, 2018a; 2018b). They came to the conclusion that when it comes to foreign markets, the Polish furniture brand is mostly known to intermediaries and is intrinsically linked with the idea of low price, which was probably already sensed by the industry (PARP, 2018b). The brand image of "cheap yet solid" is the reason why the Polish furniture is being massively ordered, but at the same time it often contributes to the low profitability the sector.

The agency prepared a brand strategy that should enhance the recognition of the Polish national brand as well as contribute to the favorable change of business models. Toward the end of the process, three competing brand concepts were tested – concept A – highlighting the idea of a smart design, concept B – underlining ecological features and concept C – focused on communicating high quality. The winning concept was one of "Smart furniture made in Poland."

The vision of the newly minted brand of Polish furniture is built around the concept of "smart design," that is, the kind of design that embraces multi-functionality of the furniture pieces and their synergy with electronic devices. The state agency responsible for the project shared the full documentation of the strategy-building process to make future users aware of traps and shortcomings of various paths, including the one that was selected as final. A private marketing agency provided the materials that can be now used by the Polish furniture producers in their promotion abroad.

---

[6] https://mediapfr.prowly.com/44027-polish-development-fund-has-developed-a-new-instrument-export-accelerator-for-the-furniture-industry visited on February 28, 2022.

3.6.5 The Go-to Brand Program

The common national brand was designed to support the promotion of the entire furniture industry, but the main beneficiaries were SMEs that could hardly afford their own branding campaigns. Yet there was also another initiative resulting from the SRD, one that supported the marketing efforts, namely the "Go-to Brand" project.[7] It was targeted at the enterprises from the sectors listed as prospective (including the furniture industry) and it consisted of financial grants that could be spent on a variety of promotional actions abroad (fair participation, paid ads, consulting etc.). The program was well received by the branch; it was mostly praised for its elasticity and low level of own contribution.

3.7 The Culture

The industry has a strong cultural specificity. It is shaped by the basic facts about the furniture firms in Poland (mostly family firms are run by the first or second generation of entrepreneurs built from scratch with no foreign capital) and by the quite intensive social life that the representatives of the industry lead.

3.7.1 Family Firms

Most of the furniture producers are family firms or started as such. Many large firms hold the name of the founder, and the majority of top-management members share the same family name. This leaves a particular mark on the company's culture, even when they grow big.

In the case of many family furniture companies, it took them too long to professionalize strategic management or the human capital management processes. The informal hierarchy and chain-of-command (family members vs the rest of the firm) might have been a way of conflict-solving and decision-making for years. On the other hand, these companies have strong cultural identity, as they have been run in a consistent manner for years.

Oftentimes the founding family is personally attached to the company and this warm, personal attitude is somehow contagious. It spills over to relations within the firm but also within the whole industry. The language that is spoken at the industry meeting isn't just the instrumental language of a liberal economy. This phenomenon was particularly visible during the 2020 COVID-19 pandemic, when the Chamber of Commerce held online meetings, where apart from the typical business issues (e.g. governmental shield program), the entrepreneurs would console and support each other in a very friendly and personal manner.

---

[7] www.parp.gov.pl/component/grants/grants/go-to-brand-expo-2020 visited on February 28, 2022.

Many furniture companies are also active in philanthropic projects. Bathroom furniture leader Deftrans and the wood furniture giant Vox run their own educational projects (an elementary school and a university, respectively); Nowy Styl, Szynaka Meble, Black Red White or Forte and many others regularly support various charity projects in their respective regions. There are also many examples of grass-root initiatives of helping out co-workers or compatriots in trouble. In the long interview about his career, Leszek Wójcik, the founder of one of the leading Polish furniture firms, recalls a moment when his production halls burned down in a massive fire and he experiences solidarity from various business partners. "The factories producing wood panels, all the factories in Poland, provided the materials. They didn't ask for money. [...] In that misfortune, as I said, a bond was formed, my trust in people, that no one left me in that misfortune" (Hryniewicki, 2015: 403).

3.7.2 The Public Square of the Industry

The people from the industry have a social life of their own that include meetings, media, rituals, stories and celebrities.

First, there is the Polish Chamber of Commerce of Furniture Manufacturers (Ogólnopolska Izba Gospodarcza Producentów Mebli) that has become a leading voice of the industry in dialogue with the government. As one can imagine, some founders and executives of the biggest companies are more active in the association, some remain silent and some do not belong at all. And yet, the activity of the Chamber is quite visible and impactful.

The industry gathers regularly at various events: fairs, conferences, galas and others. Often the business-oriented fairs are accompanied by social meetings or conferences. This is the case with an annual meeting of women in the (male-dominated) Polish furniture industry organized by the Chamber of Commerce as an event accompanying the DREMA fair in Poznan. Sometimes the major players of the industry meet at panels dedicated to the industry during some more general conferences or economic forums.

The most important domestic fairs for the branch include the Warsaw Home & Contract or Meble Polska and DREMA in Poznan. As for international fairs, the main events in Cologne (Orgatec and IMM) as well as the Salone del Mobile in Milano are the most prestigious ones. Only a few Polish firms decide to present there regularly.

Obviously, the ecosystem includes analytical and consulting services. When it comes to the most important domestic branch reports, they are supplied by governmental or state-owned institutions: the PKO BP Bank, Pekao SA Bank, The Polish Development Fund (PFR), the Polish Investment and Trade Agency.

Private consultancies sometimes also take interest in furniture production and publish their own reports – the example being KPMG. There are consultancies specializing in the furniture industry, the most prominent being B+R STUDIO Tomasz Wiktorski.

There is also a special role which the academics play in the community. There are two major wood technology departments in Poland (in Warsaw and Poznan) and the faculty collaborates closely with the industry and its various bodies, such as the council of the Chamber of Commerce. Academic and practitioners have collaborated in various R&D projects. The history of the branch has also been preserved thanks to the efforts of the associated academics referenced to in the second section.

The branch has its own magazines, the biggest being Biznes Meblowy, Meble Plus, Meble News and Biznes Meble. The latter is a part of a larger conglomerate that includes an online shop (meble.pl), a publishing house and an institution granting a prestigious prize – the diamond of the furniture industry (Diament Meblarstwa). Other competitions include The man/woman of the decade or The product of the year. It is also a prestigious thing to end up on the cover of the Biznes Meble magazine.

Moreover, there are prizes given in categories loosely connected with the furniture industry, but widely recognized as prestigious. To mention just a few, there is the Red Dot Award for design, Ernst and Young prize for the entrepreneur of the year, or Design Alive Awards in various categories.

3.8 Human Capital

The furniture industry in Poland has built its strong position partially thanks to low labor costs. Based on a 2019 work efficiency analysis of the furniture industry in selected EU countries, Denmark has the highest income per employee, amounting to EUR 239,000. Finland is in second place with the result of EUR 193,000. In turn, Sweden is in third place, with a slightly worse result at EUR 181,000. As for Poland, the revenues per employee amounted to over EUR 61.2 thousand. With average personnel costs per employee being still relatively low in Poland, the employee efficiency ratio (average revenues/costs per one employee) is the highest among EU countries (B+R STUDIO Tomasz Wiktorski, 2022). Paradoxically, the better off the Polish economy is, the more this source of competitive advantage become problematic.

Average pay continues to rise. The period of economic prosperity changed the labor market, and so did the legislation that raised the minimum pay. Another problem is workforce scarcity. This is a general problem but has some industry-specific aspects. Due to demographic changes the number of people of working age shrinks consistently. This gap has not yet closed with the influx of immigrant workers, although in 2021 foreign employees accounted for over 5% of the social insurance payers. The demand for furniture from Poland entails the demand for new employees.

 Despite the rapid automatization of the industrial production of furniture in Poland, it is still labor-intensive. As far as upholstered furniture is concerned, much work must be done manually by a skilled worker, unless the producer has the most recent, expensive Industry 4.0-type technology at their disposal. It takes at least two years to train an upholsterer. It takes even longer when one is supposed to work with leather. In companies specializing in custom-made, small batch production, the demand for professionals is even higher and the loss of key personnel potentially critical. Unfortunately, fewer and fewer people wish to pursue their career in furniture-related craft or production.

 The cost and availability of human capital has become one of the key factors shaping the competitiveness of the Polish furniture producers. The collaboration with vocational schools and rich benefit packages for immigrant workers, especially from Ukraine, are the industry's ways of alleviating human capital shortages.

4 The Business Models and Value Drivers

4.1 The Business Models

The shape of a business model is the outcome of managerial imagination and agency executed in given circumstances, as "the BM is at the point of convergence of the many constraints that arise in the firm's different universes of activity and knowing" (Spender, 2014: 497). In the case of the furniture industry, one of the decisive constraints is the shape of the value chain that the firm enters. In Section 4.1.1 we reconstruct four main types of business models present within the furniture industry, depending on the role of the firm in the value chain.

4.1.1 Subcontracting Business Models

Production is at the core of the dominant business model among Polish furniture companies. Most of them excel primarily in manufacturing – on time and with good quality-to-price ratio. The surrounding production ecosystem has been developing for three decades and provides a solid ground for competitive advantage. The firms operating in this type of a business model enter domestic or global value chains selling their production capacity and becoming subcontractors to lead firms that play the role of the value chain integrator. The subcontractor is responsible for the manufacturing of a product according to the so-called "entrusted designs" – detailed specifications received from the buyer.

The profitability of such business models depends on cost-efficiency and bargaining power based on the value proposition for the buyer. If the main criterion for an international buyer is price, Poland is less and less a go-to option, because producers from China, Vietnam or even Bulgaria or Romania is more competitive in this respect. However, there are still Polish firms that due to the lack of rare skills follow a path of very asymmetrical relations with their buyers (Gereffi, Humprey & Sturgeon, 2005). With high labor costs and material costs their margins oscillate around 2% – hardly the survival level.

Nevertheless, there are thriving companies operating within the subcontracting framework. Large production capacity, rare skills – whether based on technology or on human capital – constitute a viable value proposition and may significantly increase the margins of a subcontractor. A common practice for smaller firms is to focus on a niche (medical furniture, solid wood pieces, furniture of combined materials, etc.) and offer high-quality services. Thanks to knowledge-sharing within the Polish clusters, many firms moved from "the cheapest subcontractor" toward more knowledge-intensive and, therefore, more balanced positions in the value chains.

4.1.2 Proprietary Brand Business Model

Having established their position as manufacturer, some firms expand beyond production and take over further stages of the value chain. This move involves development of marketing capabilities and promotion of a brand name as well as collaboration with designers. This change within the business model requires a serious mental and operational shift in the company. The core of this business model is shifted from production to marketing. The step from subcontracting to brand building has been usually linked with opening a firm to the modern management thought and hiring people from outside of the furniture family to professionalize the processes.

Moving from the subcontracting model to the brand-centered business model is like moving from a two- to five-dimensional system. Suddenly there are more "knowledge absences" (Spender, 2014) – on an everyday basis the strategists experience not only sheer ignorance (not knowing something that is knowable, for example, the latest environmental regulation of the EU), but also incommensurability (not being able to construct a coherent mental model of the different aspects of reality) and indeterminacy (unpredictability of human decisions) (Spender, 2014).

Within this general model there are few different options one can take. First of all, depending on the market, furniture might be sold under a B2B or a B2C brand. These situations differ significantly and require different marketing strategies.

Some firms export their furniture to Germany under a B2B brand (this is the most common paradigm in that market) but at the same time they build a B2C brand for other markets, especially the domestic one. Another option is to combine the brand name development with subcontracting assignments in order to fully exploit the production capacities especially in the transition period.

4.1.3 Innovative Business Models

Some companies take a step further and not only integrate the entire value chain but they also redefine the rules of the game and fundamentally innovate their business model by rethinking the entire philosophy of furniture production and distribution.

One such example can be Nowy Styl Company. When the company reached a certain level of growth and operational excellence, the executive team decided to redefine the focus of the firm from furniture production and marketing to the service of office solutions provision. The change was very radical and entailed "abandonment" of numerous previous clients. Another grand business model innovator is the Tylko company. The heart of their business model is design, customization and client interface; production is treated as a commodity and outsourced. The cases of both companies are described in Section 5.

4.1.4 The Market Type Value Chain

The fourth type of business model is rare but interesting from a strategic point of view. The niche of custom-made home furniture constructions fitting a particular space, such as bookshelves, wardrobes, kitchen furniture is the space where no clear asymmetry of relations has been established. Instead, arm's-length transactions between various value-adding actors dominate. This is a small sector, estimated at 2–3% of the domestic market. According to Gereffi, Humprey and Sturgeon (2005), the market type of value chain coordination dominates when transactions can be easily codified, product specifications are relatively simple and suppliers have the capability to make products with little input from buyers. This is the case in this particular niche.

In the business model the individual integrators (usually micro-firms) get in contact with end-customers and offer a comprehensive service, starting from measurement of the space and simple design of the product (out of standardized modules) up to the assembly and installation. The integrator buys standardized component parts from wholesalers or producers and commissions the customized cutting and drilling of the wood-based panels. Every element can be bought from different sellers due to the widespread system of codification that makes the components interchangeable.

There have been attempts to strengthen the role of various elements of the value chain in this segment, thus moving it away from the market coordination model toward more asymmetrical relations. The question is, who will gain the power, and how?

Particularly interesting is the attempt of the large wholesalers of furniture component parts to try to bind the individual integrators to themselves. They do this by offering a comprehensive solution to the integrators. A dedicated design app permits full automatization of the process; that is, the integrator (buyer) may design the piece and send the data directly to the automatized production machines. The whole process is smooth and fast. Such a business model benefits the integrators in multiple ways and at the same time makes it less likely for them to be willing to switch the supplier. With time this may lead to the dominating position of the wholesalers, who would manage to "lock-in" a number of individual integrators.

Another story of gaining a significant competitive advantage in the sector of custom-made home furniture is the Komandor brand. It belongs to a furniture firm established in 1992 offering custom-made wardrobes with sliding doors. Thanks to high-quality, advanced technological solutions and a consistent strategy, the company dominated this market niche on the Polish market and the brand name became a synonym for a type of furniture, regardless of the producer. The corporation is very successful, has its own distribution network in Poland and sells to forty-four countries on four continents, with particularly strong relations in Asia.

4.2 Value Drivers

4.2.1 Brand

One of the measures of the power of a brand in the furniture industry is the average export price of 100 kilograms of furniture. The result achieved by the Polish producers in 2020 (EUR 259) was the second lowest result in the European Union. The EU average was EUR 375; Italy had an average of EUR 424 and Germany, EUR 466 (Pekao SA, 2021). The fact that Poland sells below the average price is not surprising, given that the main competitive advantage of the majority of Polish furniture firms is their low price. The situation cannot be improved overnight, but the industry hopes to slowly abandon this market segment and achieve some convergence of selling prices to those in the EU.

Since the price gap is believed to be marketing based, the industry seeks marketing methods to close it. For the large subcontractors there are two most common approaches. One is to gain value by building recognition among the distributors. The brand is promoted mostly through professional channels and during international fairs. Recognition among intermediaries allows them to "justify" higher prices while staying in the same relational business model. The other way, however, consists of moving toward an integrated business model. In this case a typical trajectory consists of developing a brand targeted to individual users on the domestic market, while still working as a subcontractor on the international markets. In this way a firm may gradually gain the marketing knowhow required to operate in the integrated business model.

Once a firm encompasses the entire value chain, marketing strategy becomes one of the key factors shaping the business model. Brand identity must be aligned with all the other aspects of the business model such as product design, distribution and production. Sometimes this alignment is achieved by construction of the right narrative around the existing business. Here the brand may add some value to the project, but the return on the money invested in marketing might as well be moderate.

Sometimes, however, the brand is given priority and the business model is built around a carefully crafted marketing strategy, often relying on e-commerce, augmented reality technology and a strong social media presence. All the other aspects of the business are considered secondary and modified accordingly. There are cases of furniture firms that share this kind of philosophy and have achieved a pace of growth far exceeding their peers with a more conservative marketing approach. One of the examples can be noo.ma brand – a fast growing, e-commerce-based Polish brand selling its furniture to the EU or Tylko – one of the most valuable Polish startups described in Section 5.

One of the strong trends in marketing is creation of a strong brand recognition among interior design professionals: architects, developers and the like. This is the go-to element of marketing strategy among workplace furniture producers, but it is also gaining popularity among home furniture makers. A loyalty program targeted at professionals has gradually become a natural element of sales strategy for all the integrated furniture businesses.

4.2.2 Industry 4.0

While some Polish furniture firms still struggle to introduce any digital solutions in production, many other enterprises are heading toward the Industry 4.0 standard of manufacturing. This standard assumes digital integration of the value chain knowledge flow (e.g. information from customers sent directly to the manufacturing machinery), the use of autonomous and collaborative robots, implementation of lean production principles as well as training personnel to collaborate smoothly with machines.

Industry 4.0 is much more than a solution to human capital shortages and increasing labor costs – it is a complex philosophy of production that potentially allows for major cost-cutting, increased efficiency and minimization of various types of waste throughout the value chain. Such a production standard opens up new possibilities for product innovation and customization. The technology available today allows industry to minimize the tension between the trend to large-scale production and the agility that allows for small-batch, highly customized production in one factory.

Due to high investment costs and the necessity to integrate the entire value chain under one umbrella system, such solutions are being implemented in either integrated or hierarchical business models. For subcontractors, technological integration with the buyers' systems might become problematic. Since there is no universal IT standard, investment in a certain type of technology by the subcontracting firms might cause an asset specificity and result in the firms slipping into a captive relationship with their buyers.

4.2.3 Consolidation, Mergers and Acquisitions

One of the major value drivers discussed within the industry is horizontal and vertical consolidation and foreign acquisitions.

While there may be some niche segments where small and medium companies thrive, in the mainstream furniture industry the key to profitability is cost-cutting through the economy of scale. Only large entities can afford state-of-the-art technology (the Industry 4.0 standard) and present a strong negotiating position with large buyers. The fragmentation of the Polish furniture industry is an important obstacle in achieving the latter.

There are attempts to consolidate on the side of small and medium companies in some regional clusters. Usually, they form an umbrella entity that loosely connects the firms and allows negotiations on the local level (energy costs, materials, etc.). This is not a type of consolidation that could bring a breakthrough in profitability, however.

Real, large-scale mergers do not happen within the Polish furniture industry. A part of the reason why this is the case is the fact that they remain family firms. It is extremely difficult to merge family companies, because of the strong emotional surplus that accompanies such transactions. However, the near future may bring some novelties in this respect. In June 2022 it was announced that the Austrian furniture giant XXXLutz would acquire 50% of Black Red White, one of the largest Polish furniture enterprises with their own multichannel distribution system.

The acquisitions that seem particularly desirable for Polish producers are foreign ones. The famous case of Nowy Styl Group (described in detail in Section 5), which acquired strong German and French brands, has inspired Polish entrepreneurs not only in the furniture industry. Such an expansion, though risky, allows a company to quickly enter a market with their own brand without the lonesome and costly process of constructing one from scratch.

4.2.4 Big Partners and New Markets

The largest markets that Polish furniture producers sell to are stagnant and mature. The best example is the German market, where the competition is dense, and the furniture trade is highly structured and difficult to enter for newcomers. Therefore, there are two main strategies used by the producers to secure markets for their goods: building strong relations with powerful intermediaries in the current sales market, and entering new markets.

The first strategy is particularly appealing to those who do not wish to switch entirely to the integrated, hierarchical business model (encompassing the entire value chain), but who prefer to grow while focusing on the core competence of production in the subcontracting business model. Such companies seek to secure an agreement with large distributors, such as the German purchasing groups (e.g. Bega, VME Union GmbH or Giga Lutz) or the international retailer IKEA. Contracts with such strong partners are only available for the large, technologically advanced producers such as Szynaka, Forte, Com40 or Black Red White. Smaller firms usually sell to the domestic market or become subcontractors to larger firms that have access to distribution channels.

When it comes to new markets, one option is geographical. Firms which cannot achieve an expected level of sales on the default foreign markets (Germany, Czech Republic, Great Britain) or which seek to promote their own brand, which is rather difficult on the European market, look to other, more distant directions. As was presented in the second section (in the section about export), the industry, with the help of the Polish government, has been making a collective effort to open trade routes to the USA, Middle East and Kazakhstan.

In contrast, SMEs, however, try to follow the path of many Italian boutique firms, which prosper quite well despite their moderate size. Such firms often start on the local market looking for a niche – crafted solid wood furniture, short-series luxury lines, contracts for elegant stores, etc. Such firms often derive their inspiration from the traditions of the Polish woodworking craft. For now, such firms have managed to make a good living. In Section 5, the cases of Miloni and RC Design present unique business models built around the market niche.

4.2.5 E-commerce and Omnichannel

Statistically speaking, the furniture industry is lagging behind other areas of retail, when it comes to e-commerce. One can clearly see, however, that online furniture shopping has been trending for some time: over the past few years, furniture has become one of the fastest-growing segments in the overall retail e-commerce industry. As in the case of other industries, e-commerce has the potential to turn the market upside down and to make today's leading retailers obsolete, if they do not surf on this wave.

The reason why e-commerce has such a revolutionary potential is simple – today's technology makes it possible to reach the end customer without any help from distributors, no matter how prominent they may be. Younger users have become used to the customer experience that online shopping provides and they seek it in new areas of their lives. In 2019, 12% of furniture sales in the world were generated by online stores. It is projected that the value will increase to the level of 15% in 2023 (PKO BP, 2021). There are two technological advances that together create prospects for a bright future for furniture e-commerce: Augmented Reality (AR) technology and personalized online marketing.

Augmented Reality technology has made it possible to view furniture projected into a designated space on the screen of a smartphone. Many retailers offer this service through dedicated apps or, most recently – even without them (web-native versions). The fear of buying a piece of furniture that would be a complete mismatch for the style and size of the space has thus been alleviated. The analytical tools that allow personalized marketing make the customer experience even better, by providing them with customized ads that respond, for example, to the customer's Pinterest activity. In addition, social media provide inspiration and advice as well as a powerful promotional platform.

For Polish furniture producers, e-commerce might become a frontier where every settler is equal and years of experience and tradition lose their defining power. The recognition of a brand in the physical world may not necessarily translate into similar recognition in the virtual world. Online marketing opens a common ground and an opportunity for synergy with the startup community. A good example of such synergetic collaboration is Lofty, a bot developed by a Polish startup that uses artificial intelligence to offer a free interior design service to individual users. The startup partners up with various producers and online retailers to provide a wide range of available products.[8]

There is also a marketing trend targeted at those more conservative clients who do shop online, but when it comes to furniture, prefer to physically touch

---

[8] https://innpoland.pl/164369,bot-za-darmo-zaaranzuje-wnetrze-startup-lofty-wirtualny-projektant visited on May 30, 2022.

and see a piece of furniture and material option samples before purchase. The practice of omnichannel furniture marketing might creatively link showrooms and physical stores, e-commerce and social media presence to create a personalized customer experience.

4.2.6 Attached Services

Enriching the physical product with the element of a service is a value driver well known in many industries. In the furniture industry additional services may take several different forms.

The most common is customization of a catalogue, mass-produced product. The customer may choose between various options of colors, fabrics, fillings, etc. This is a particularly common feature in the case of upholstered furniture. From the producer's perspective, customization requires a careful process management. Personalization requires a reliable communication system between the customer, the seller and the producer in order to avoid mistakes and waste. Customization may cause disruption in the production process, so this service can be offered only by manufacturers at a certain level of organizational maturity.

The second most common type is a comprehensive service that includes interior design and furnishing of a space. This kind of service is offered by advanced workplace furniture producers, but it is also sometimes offered on the home furniture market. The service may be limited to basic consulting, or it may be a turnkey project encompassing the entire process from thorough research into the particular needs of a customer, through design to production and assembly of all the elements. The latter type of contracts are gaining in popularity, reinforced by the trend toward the "homification" of office space as a part of employer branding.

As the turnkey contracts become more frequent, we may observe a convergence of various businesses related to interior design. For example, real estate agencies that offer offices for lease take responsibility for the adjustment of the space to the needs of a given customer. Therefore, they act as a contractor that hires the ethnographers (to understand the needs of the employees who will occupy the space), designers and furniture providers. The key to the value capture game that is being played here is to gain direct access to the customer and to become the turnkey contractor who hires everyone else. So far, the real estate agencies seem to be leading the way.

One can also notice, especially on the office-furniture market, the innovative trend of furniture-as-a-service. Instead of purchasing furniture for an office (or less frequently – for a home) the customer may decide to buy a subscription in the form of operational lease and pay only for the period of time when they utilize the product. The solution is present worldwide, but not particularly common. Moreover, it is hardly ever the furniture producer that provides the service (the exception being, e.g., IKEA).

Another trending service is connected with the idea of a smart home. Furniture integrated with digitally controlled electronic devices is still a rare type of product, but interest seems to be growing. The umbrella marketing strategy commissioned by the government agency for the Polish furniture industry is based on the slogan "Smart furniture made in Poland." It turns out that the idea of "smart" is less associated with the multifunctionality of the furniture or its ergonomics, as the experts assumed, but smart furniture is expected to smoothly fit into the whole smart home idea which integrates the virtual and the material world.

4.2.7 Design

The firms operating fully within the subcontracting business model do not engage in the design process. However, for the firms operating partially or fully within the integrated business model, the design might be a powerful value driver, especially when coupled with effective marketing.

In the couple of years directly following the fall of Communism, most Polish furniture firms either worked with designs provided by the contractor or produced basic furniture designed ad hoc, often by copying projects known from trade fairs or foreign catalogues. The tradition of design existed in Poland. There were even some examples of exquisite design, also in the realm of mass production like the famous 366 armchair designed by Józef Chierowski, produced continuously for over two decades.

And yet traditional Polish design did not quite influence the reality of the furniture industry in capitalist Poland. The main reasons for this were cultural and practical ones. Famous Polish designers usually were professors of Fine Art Academies, members of the intelligentsia, closed in their own circle or collaborating with big state-run industry. There were hardly any places or circles where they could meet and get to know the entrepreneurs that built the strength of the domestic furniture industry. They belonged to quite different worlds culturally, geographically and sociologically. Their projects were often bold and artistic, but not suited for mass production. Moreover, the enormous demand for Polish furniture in the former Soviet Union in the early 1990s was not connected with quality design. When the industry reoriented toward German customers, there was hardly any interest in local design.

In the years to come a new generation of Polish designers entered the market, and quite many gained international recognition, the most prominent examples being Oskar Zięta, Tomek Rygalik, Maja Ganaszyniec, Krystian Kowalski, Piotr Kuchciński, Jan Kochański and Tomasz Augustyniak. Slowly the bridges between the world of design and the industry were built. Nowadays the projects of the aforementioned designers are often mass-produced by the best Polish brands and the synergetic effect of that collaboration is visible. There are brands that specialize in top-shelf Polish design – Noti company, described in detail in Section 5, being a good example. Piotr Voelkel, the founder and co-owner of the Vox Capital group, one of the largest furniture companies in Poland, and SWPS University established a department of design called the School of Form to educate young designers in direct collaboration with various industries.

In other words, high-quality design is widely available for the Polish firms that want to engage in this kind of collaboration. Now a vital goal should be to boost the brands and entire business models with high-quality design.

4.2.8 Operational Excellence

Growing companies that expand their business models beyond production gain a lot by focusing on operational excellence and implementing the habit of constant improvement. This usually requires a clearly designed organizational structure and professionalized management processes.

As has been repeatedly underscored, a vast majority of Polish furniture firms were founded and run as family enterprises. Among many features that this situation entails, there is also a certain reluctance to fully apply modern management systems and norms in areas other than production or sales. Many family firms stop half way, trying to introduce state-of-the-art, technologically supported management systems, while keeping the back door of informal coordination open, should they need it. This is particularly visible in human capital management.

Well-designed, customized systems that support strategic management, human capital development, customer relations, marketing and sales may work as catalysts to permit firms to take full advantage of their strengths in all business areas. This is especially valid in the case of firms that operate with integrated business models, where synergy between various types of activity is the key to success.

5 Case Studies

5.1 Nowy Styl

Nowy Styl is one of the most successful Polish furniture companies. Established in 1992 by two brothers, Adam and Jerzy Krzanowski, the company is now a multinational player selling to over 100 countries and number one on the

European market of office chairs as well as one of the top global providers of comprehensive solutions for offices and public spaces.

The trajectory of early development of Nowy Styl is akin to other furniture producers that managed to grow big. Yet there are some differences that may seem minor, yet when combined they contributed to a quite different outcome. Over the course of time the Krzanowski brothers made a number of contentious, pivotal decisions that made their business grow into a global player and an international brand, as opposed to successful, yet local, businesses that simply rode the wave of opportunities of the political transition era skillfully. In other words, Nowy Styl grew much above the level of organic development of the entire furniture industry in the region.

5.1.1 A (Slightly Different) Beginning

It is hard to present a psychologically plausible reconstruction of the unique entrepreneurial spirit of the Krzanowski brothers. It does not seem to run in the family – their parents both worked in a state-owned glass factory in the peripheral, middle-sized town of Krosno. One attempt to open an ice cream shop in the family house ended badly and could have become a trauma rather than an energizing memory (Hryniewicki, 2015: 94–95). Yet for some reason both Adam and Jerzy Krzanowski abandoned the dominant recipe for success in life (i.e. academic achievements at school and meticulous work for a stable employer) and found their own path – pioneering and adventurous.

Both brothers earned their first wages in their early teen years by taking pictures of crashed cars for their uncle – an insurance company appraiser. They did not seem to care for school much. Jerzy recalls that when picking a secondary school for himself, he looked for a place where he would study as little as possible and have time to do business. He ended up as a student in a gastronomic school, skipping over 200 hours of classes each semester. But he used this time to travel to Turkey and West Berlin to smuggle goods to communist Poland and sell them with a 100% margin (Hryniewicki, 2015: 98–100). After a short episode of working for an Israeli restaurant, Jerzy decided to start his own cafe in Krosno. Yet neither this business nor another innovative idea (the first bridal gown rental in Krosno) turned out to be successful.

Around the same time Adam, the older of the brothers, took a year off from university and left for the United States to earn some money. He ended up unloading trucks at the chair manufacturing company called Whyte. Adam gets the idea that the chair manufacturing business could be profitable in Poland, so he sends to his brother Jerzy some pictures of the furniture produced by Whyte – not even a catalogue, just some pictures. Jerzy showed these pictures to local furniture retailers for advice and got excited about the project. Adam was bold enough to talk to the Whyte owners – Henry and Roland Stern – about investing in a new business in Poland. The Sterns agree. In 1992 the Nowy Styl company was established (Hryniewicki, 2015).

This story differs from those of other Polish furniture blockbusters on many occasions, the first and prominent part is the American investor. Indeed, at the early stage, not only the initial investment, but also the know-how and guarantees for the Italian suppliers that the Sterns provided helped the Krzanowski brothers accelerate the growth curve of Nowy Styl. The growth was indeed exponential.

The first three types of chairs were made in 1992 at a manufacturing site that stank with fertilizers and did not even have a proper heating, not to mention restrooms (Hryniewicki, 2015: 118). It took Nowy Styl half a year to move to a 3,000-square-meter hall at the Krosno airport. The space became too small after another year.

The business model was both simple and bold. At the beginning, the chairs were simply assembled of the parts imported from Italy. The demand was great and the market deep. Oddly, the shape of the metal chairs offered resembled that of the traditional bentwood products made by Thonet Brothers since the nineteenth century. But the metal chairs – while cheaper in production – were considered more modern and stylish, and so their selling price was double that of the bentwood chairs, making it possible to achieve three-digit margins. Soon Nowy Styl replaced the imported parts with their own production and stood out among the competitors who kept importing everything. Thanks to the savings made through the insourcing of production, Nowy Styl stood out from the competition by offering a wider range of products (e.g. different colors of upholstery) for less, while keeping the enormous margins. Soon the company introduced their bestselling product – the swivel chair. The inflow of cash was incredible, but the brothers resisted the temptation to monetize the success and made sure that the larger share of the income was being reinvested. In the first few years the firm grew at a pace of over 1000% a year (Hryniewicki, 2015: 126). At some point the company did not have any real domestic competitor – no one but the Italians could measure up to Nowy Styl.

5.1.2 The first stage of European expansion (1995–2006)

Russia and Ukraine

The first foreign markets that the company grew on were that of Russia and Ukraine. As early as 1995 Nowy Styl appeared at the largest furniture fair in Moscow presenting twenty-five models of chairs (Hryniewicki, 2015: 131).

The Eastern market was deep and easy – the dominant business model was very safe for the Polish producer: Russian clients would first transfer money to their account, and when the batch was ready, they would send their own transport to pick up the cargo. The expectations concerning quality were moderate; Russian clients appreciated the prices that were significantly lower than those offered in Italy.

The Eastern market was crucial for Nowy Styl in the first decade, so the company entered a partnership and started production in Kharkov (Ukraine) as well as in Bilgorod in Russia. Their strong presence on the Eastern market, relatively independent from the Western economy, was instrumental in the successful overcoming of the financial crisis of 2008–2009 (Hryniewicki, 2015).

Western Europe

After their great success in the East, Nowy Styl sought to enter the largest Western-European markets: Germany and France. Like most of the rising stars of the Polish furniture industry, Nowy Styl took part in the prestigious ORGATEC fair in Cologne for the first time in 1996. The Western European market was quite different from the eastern one. There, distribution networks were complex and petrified, competition was dense and the standards of quality and overall customer care – very high. At the early stage, the company could only compete on price. It took years of experience and contacts to be able to sell products to more demanding customers in the middle and upper market segments.

5.1.3 Strategic Reorientation (2006–2008)

Nowy Styl built its brand as a producer of chairs. In the early 2000s the company sought ways to rise above the economic segment and compete on features other than price. The Krzanowski brothers decided to enter a long-term collaboration with an Austrian firm, Bene Office Solution. As Bene's subcontractor, Nowy Styl got a quick lesson in the requirements of the Western markets. Bene would send their engineers and designers to Poland to ensure the quality and aesthetics of the chairs produced, as well as the high level of service and timeliness of deliveries (Latusek-Jurczak, 2017).

A fruitful cooperation resulted in the creation of a new company in Poland controlled by both partners – Bene-Nowy Styl. Bene brought their know-how about office furnishing that Nowy Styl adjusted to the Central and Eastern European needs. Collaborating with Bene, Nowy Styl had the chance to engage in a new type of activity – providing comprehensive furnishing solutions for offices. After a couple of years of such collaboration, Nowy Styl was ready to take up independent activity in the new segment. Bene Office Furniture agreed to sell their shares in Bene-Nowy Styl to the partner in 2006 (Latusek-Jurczak, 2017).

This is when the Krzanowski brothers decided to conduct a strategic reorientation of the company. Until that point, they only sold chairs. Meanwhile, statistics showed that chairs accounted for only 30% of the value of office furnishings, and customers were also interested in buying other office furniture. The firm decided to expand their assortment. The decision was quite risky. First, it required a shift in production. The next risks were connected with the clients. Until that point a large part of Nowy Styl's customers were furniture manufacturers. Entering the segment of comprehensive office solutions meant the losing those clients without a guarantee of gaining new ones (Latusek-Jurczak, 2017).

The strategic reorientation in the realm of products required an adequate branding policy. Until this point, Nowy Styl brand had been associated with an economical and widely available segment. The new strategy consisted not only in broadening the portfolio of products, but in assuming a new firm identity and in making an important change in distribution policy. In the new strategy, architects played an important role as an intermediary between the client and the firm. In order to make their products attractive to architects, Nowy Styl had to build a new brand, unburdened of the economic segment associations. This is how the BN Office Solutions brand was created. It became the symbol of the company's strategic reorientation (Latusek-Jurczak, 2017).

5.1.4 The New Management Model (2008)

The rapid expansion of the firm paired with the strategic reorientation from "office chair manufacturer" to "comprehensive office solution provider" exposed some flaws in the management system.

Nowy Styl consisted of the Polish parent company and many distribution subsidiaries abroad (the number of which varied from a dozen to several dozen), each with its own management board and each focused on its own financial result. There were no incentives for the daughter companies to regard the interest of the entire group. The subsidiaries were treated as regular contractors, so every time prices were negotiated, the parties had divergent interests. This led to tensions and delays (Latusek-Jurczak, 2017).

Another problem with the structure of the group was its fragmentation and frequent overlaps of functions and responsibilities among the companies in the group. The Krzanowski brothers would make the most important decisions in the company, although they formally held the function of the proxies.

The prerogatives and responsibilities of the actual management board were unclear and volatile (Hryniewicki, 2015).

In 2008, Adam and Jerzy decided to reorganize the company and eventually transform it into an integrated multinational entity with a strong management board and deeply integrated and optimized internal processes. The daughter companies lost some of their independence, but the new incentive system aligned their interests with that of the parent company and the centralized management functions were quickly optimized (Latusek-Jurczak, 2017). Adam and Jerzy Krzanowski entered the new Management Board together with some newly hired specialists skilled in various aspects of corporate management (Hryniewicki, 2015).

This reorganization created a solid ground for another set of pivotal activities in the upcoming decade – a series of international acquisitions.

5.1.5 Expansion by Acquisition

In 2011 Nowy Styl took over Bavaria-based Sato Office, a German manufacturer of ergonomic chairs under the brand Grammer Office (Hryniewicki, 2015). The Greek owners of Sato ware the Nowy Styl clients – when the situation in the Greek mother firm became dire, the owners decided to sell the German subsidiary.

In 2013 another German company, a manufacturer of office furniture, chairs, armchairs and sofas – Rohde & Grahl – was acquired.[9] The firm enjoyed a strong presence and recognition on the German as well as Dutch market. There was a very humane element to this story. The owner and the founder of the company – Mr. Rohde – wanted to retire and did not have a proper heir to pass the company on to, but he did not want his heritage to end up in the wrong hands. Observing the successful acquisition of Sato Office, he believed that Nowy Styl would be the right choice (Hryniewicki, 2015). The Krzanowski brothers proved him right. One year after the acquisition, the Rohde & Grahl company recorded an increase in sales revenue of approximately 20%.

The integration of both acquired companies into Nowy Styl Group has been a relatively smooth process. Local production and the number of employees have remained the same, while the IT, finances and marketing services have been taken over by the centralized units.

In 2014 Nowy Styl finalized the purchase of 50% of shares in the Turkish company TCC – The Chair Company.[10] Established in 1985, TCC specialized in production and distribution of chairs for offices, auditoriums, cinemas and

---

[9] www.expo21xx.com/news/rohde-grahl-nowy-styl-group/.

[10] www.drewno.pl/artykuly/9887,nowy-styl-kupil-udzialy-w-tureckiej-spolce.html.

stadiums. The company had a well-established position on the Turkish market as well as a network of over sixty dealers in Turkey. For many years, it has been a distributor of Grammer Office products.

In 2015 Nowy Styl acquired SITAG AG from Switzerland – a manufacturer and distributor of chairs and office furniture, a very strong brand selling not only in Switzerland but also in Austria and Germany.[11] Just like Nowy Styl, SITAG provided comprehensive interior arrangement solutions. The company was integrated into the centralized system of operations, but many aspects of its activity remained the same.

In 2018, following the dynamic growth of tourism in the Middle East, Nowy Styl Group acquired a majority stake in Stylis Dubai.[12] The minority partner was an investor with whom Nowy Styl had been cooperating in the region for over six years, furnishing twenty-one hotels in Saudi Arabia. This acquisition was a pioneering move in two respects. First, it was an attempt to increase the presence in the competitive Middle-Eastern market in countries such as Saudi Arabia, the United Arab Emirates, Qatar, Kuwait, Oman and Bahrain. Second, it was an important extension of the activity of Nowy Styl, focused thus far mainly on offices and, to lesser extent, leisure areas. There is obviously some overlap between the modern office spaces and hotels, yet this may be the beginning of a full-scale reorientation or portfolio extension in the future.

In January 2019 Nowy Styl bought Kusch + Co.[13] A German family business with roots dating back to the late 1930s, the company is a premium brand with a great product recognition among architects. With the new company, the Nowy Styl portfolio gained access to new sectors such as transportation (seats for passenger terminals) and health care.

In June 2019 Nowy Styl made another bold move acquiring the French Majencia.[14] It was the first time for Nowy Styl to take over a company in a state of liquidation – so far the Group would only buy healthy companies. Majencia, a longtime leader in the field of office furniture and arranging workspaces, had experienced financial problems for quite some time. The deal included taking over Majencia factories and employing most of its staff. The move made Nowy Styl the leader on the French market of comprehensive office solutions, but also left it with a number of unresolved human capital issues in a country famous for the strong labor unions.[15]

---

[11] https://bpcc.org.pl/contact-magazine/issues/8/categories/34/articles/264.

[12] www.paih.gov.pl/20180301/gcc_hotels_fitted_polish_style.

[13] https://nowystyl.com/en/about-us/our-history/.

[14] https://nowystyl.com/en/about-us/news/109/we-acquired-french-company-majencia/.

[15] https://ergonoma.com/2020/10/majencia-outcome-for-the-french-manufacturer-of-office-furni
      ture/.

5.1.6 Rebranding

After numerous acquisitions and joint ventures, the portfolio of brands that belonged to the Nowy Styl Group had become quite rich. In 2019 the company made an important decision to rebrand and strengthen the dominant Nowy Styl trademark. The process included the departure from using the term "Group" for an umbrella brand, first on the Polish market, then all the other markets. The refreshed Nowy Styl brand was to take over all of the identity earned by the Group. However, some brands with good international recognizability (Kusch +Co, Forum Seating) or strong local recognition (SITAG by Nowy Styl in Switzerland and Stylis Hotel Solutions in the Middle East) were kept in the portfolio; others (BN Office Solutions, Grammer Office, Rohde & Grahl) ceased to exist. The portfolio was complemented by the new SOHOS by Nowy Styl subbrand, created with the commodity market in mind. The entire change is symbolized by a new black-and-white logo of Nowy Styl.

5.1.7 The Thirty-Year-Old Nowy Styl

After the hungry years and the pandemic crisis that affected the office furniture heavily, Nowy Styl is now a strong international player. It employs over 700 people worldwide. The company has showrooms in thirty-three cities, and independent structures, facilities and offices in nineteen countries across Europe and the Middle East. The key markets include:

Germany – 33%
The Netherlands – 10%
Poland – 9%
France – 8%
Switzerland – 8%
Austria – 2%
The United Kingdom –2%
The Middle East – 2%
The rest – 26%[16]

The reported revenues (aggregate data from Nowy Styl capital group and joint venture companies operating in Ukraine, Russia, Turkey and Kazakhstan):[17]

2020 – EUR 386 million
2019 – EUR 461 million
2018 – EUR 384 million

---

[16] https://nowystyl.com/files/interactive/company-profile/EN/14/.
[17] https://nowystyl.com/files/interactive/company-profile/EN/14/.

In March 2022 the executive board of Nowy Styl announced their total withdrawal from the Russian market as a token of protest against the Russian aggression against Ukraine as well as of solidarity with the entire Ukrainian nation in general and the Ukrainian Nowy Styl employees in particular.[18]

5.2 The Szynaka Group

5.2.1 The History

Jan Szynaka, the founder of today's Szynaka group, was born in 1961. The youngest of six, he practiced carpentry in the workshop of his father – Jan Szynaka Senior. After his father's death in 1985, Jan Junior inherited the workshop, membership in a cooperative with some privileges attached, and unfinished orders for renovating local movie theatres.

The young man did not exactly follow in his father's footsteps. Jan Senior – a World War II veteran who lived under a constant threat from the communist authorities – led his workshop like a true craftsman, with a code of conduct that combined conscientiousness and some disregard for the financial side of the deal (Hryniewicki, 2015: 245). Jan Junior, in turn, kept the quality orientation of his father, as well as a sense of belonging to the community of craftsmen, but his strong entrepreneurial talent soon began to unfold and sometimes distinguished or even estranged Jan from his environment.

One such estranging quality example was Jan's growth orientation. Even when times were hard, Szynaka would reinvest the money he earned into the development of his business. It was not an obvious decision in a post-communist country with a litany of memories of an unstable history. Typically, the newly minted entrepreneurs wanted to consume while there was anything to consume. Second, in the early 1990s, when Szynaka wanted to show his products at the fair in Warsaw, he was criticized by his peers for naming himself a "manager" on the business cards. This was perceived as pride. But young Szynaka understood that he was already someone else than a craftsman (Hryniewicki, 2015: 258). When his firm grew bigger, he was also looked down upon by the former directors of the once powerful, but now declining, furniture factories. Their resentment probably went beyond the natural struggle between the generations (Hryniewicki, 2015: 265).

The time of Poland's transition to the market economy in 1989 was full of paradoxes. As someone who had started his business earlier, Jan Szynaka could not qualify for the ten-year tax exemption offered to new firms. To make the situation worse, he took an extremely expensive loan to build his first

---

[18] https://pl.nowystyl.com/pl/o-nas/aktualnosci/294/nowy-styl-solidarny-z-ukraina/.

production hall. The interest rate was as high as 70% yearly. The young entrepreneur sold most of his belongings to get rid of this burden. But he would consistently develop his business. With the new machines and space, Szynaka moved smoothly from custom-made furniture for shops and public spaces to small-batch production.

The fairs in Poznan and Warsaw opened new opportunities that the young firm seized and exploited. The number of orders grew because the demand was high. The firm's problem was not to get an order but how to increase its production power. In 1991 Jan Szynaka bought a factory hall in his hometown Lubawa from a near-bankrupt building materials manufacturer.

The next seven years were a period of unprecedented prosperity due to the enormous demand on the post-Soviet market. After the fall of the Soviet Union, new businesses sprang up like mushrooms, and they all needed furniture for their shops and offices. As a shop furniture producer, Szynaka could make a sale on everything that he was able to manufacture – up to 70% of the production volume was being exported to the East. Russian clients were solid, not very picky about quality, and they never failed to pay the bill.

The tide changed suddenly. In 1998 Russia imposed a very high duty on imported goods. Any export to Russia became senseless. Like many Polish furniture producers, Szynaka lost his main market almost overnight. The firm did not have much experience or contacts in Western Europe, nor the distribution channels that could sell the production surplus on the domestic market. Jan Szynaka chose another strategy: he turned to the international giant Swedwood (subsidiary of IKEA) and became their subcontractor. The Szynaka company already had a good reputation, a state-of the-art factory and high-class staff, so the negotiations weren't long. This was an intensive lesson in Western market standards and particularity. Schieder and Schumacher collapsed some years later, but the close collaboration with IKEA became the key factor shaping the fate of the Szynaka company. The group grew consistently, opening new production sites and logistics centers in various parts of Poland.

5.2.2 The Szynaka Group Today

In 2022 the Szynaka Group is one of the largest Polish furniture manufacturers, employing about 3,500 employees, with a turnover in 2021 amounting to approximately EUR 267 million. The production is carried out in eight plants in Poland. The total area of the facilities is over 500,000 m².[19]

The dominant business model is the focus on large-scale production in very modern and automatized plants and collaboration with giant distributors.

---

[19] www.bcc.org.pl/grupa-meblowa-szynaka-zawarla-nowa-umowe-o-wspolpracy-z-grupa-bega/.

The company and its subsidiaries are one of the key partners for IKEA, providing mostly wood furniture. The German giant the BEGA Group has the exclusive rights to market the Szynaka Group's products in Western Europe. In 2021, the BEGA Group purchased furniture with a value of EUR 72 million from the Szynaka Group.[20] Stable, long-term agreements with the leading European retailers ensure the use of the firm's enormous production capacity.

5.3 Balma and Noti

Noti brand is a spin-off of BALMA – one of the largest and most successful Polish furniture companies. Both were established by the same entrepreneur, Ryszard Balcerkiewicz, although at a different stage of his life and with a different vision (Hryniewicki, 2015).

Ryszard Balcerkiewicz started his career at the age of sixteen. Raised by a single mother, he had to leave his dream of a university education behind and took his first job while still attending a technical secondary school (Hryniewicki, 2015: 20). The young, talented and diligent man soon became a manager and set up his own family. In 1978 he decided to give up employment and establish a one-man firm producing metal tools and elements in a modest electrotechnical workshop. His products varied from small metal elements to lightning protection systems. The young entrepreneur did not hesitate to try something new, should the opportunity arise. Balcerkiewicz' real success came when he engaged in the production of computer desks in 1988. The political breakthrough of 1989 paired with the expansion of computer technologies created a high demand for such products. The simple desk made of metal and wood-based panel and designed by Balcerkiewicz himself became a bestseller in Poland. Balma grew very fast, becoming one of the leading producers of office furniture in Poland.

The factor that largely contributed to Balma's success was the ingenuity and flexibility of the founder. Balcerkiewicz managed to recognize and exploit the unprecedented opportunities of the political transition era and turned the electrotechnical workshop into a large and successful furniture company able to operate on various domestic and foreign markets. Over the course of time, he made several bold and pivotal decisions that made success possible. Among them were the decisions to regularly take part in the international furniture fair ORGATEC, to buy a large portion of land in western Poland (the region soon became highly industrialized and valuable), and to engage young and talented Polish designers in Balma's projects.

---

[20] https://biznes.meble.pl/aktualnosci,nowa-umowa-grupy-bega-i-grupy-szynaka,17879.html.

The story behind Noti brand is different. In 2005 Ryszard Balcerkiewicz stepped down from the position of the CEO of Balma and passed the steering wheel of the already large company to his son – Michał. However, when the succession process was completed, Balcerkiewicz Senior did not retire, but decided to engage in something fresh. Noti started as a small company leasing a tiny space from BALMA and supplementing the mother firm's portfolio with a set of upholstered furniture for office spaces. The new projects "appeared" without much effort. Soon the company was able to surf the wave of the new trend – the domestication of office spaces. Balma's ex-customers would turn to Noti to give their offices a homely vibe with the help of well-designed sofas or armchairs (Hryniewicki, 2015).

The firm's pace of growth was rapid – after one year there was already a need for a full-scale production hall, professional sales force, and a new strategy, distinct from that of Balma. Initially, the production was targeted at office users, but soon it turned out that there was a demand for Noti products on the home furniture market. Over the course of time, Noti would also become a contract manufacturer for interior design projects in public spaces – cinemas, hotels and restaurants.

At the early stage, the most urgent strategic challenge was that of distribution channels. Obviously, as far as office furniture was concerned, Noti would use the Balma sales network. However, a new category of clients – home users – required a new approach. Balcerkiewicz sought to collaborate with various furniture retailers, but did not close a deal. At the end of the day, Balcerkiewicz created a subbrand – Galeria Noti (Noti gallery) and opened three showrooms in Poland presenting the Noti collection with some Balma elements.

Noti was supposed to provide limited, ambitious collections of furniture signed by the rising stars of Polish design and targeted at the upper-middle class on the domestic market. Such a business model operates successfully in Italy. Balcerkiewicz was right to detect a gap on the market, but – as it turned out – he overrated its size. Contrary to predictions, the number of the showrooms in Poland not only did not grow to ten or fifteen, but it shrank to two (Hryniewicki, 2015).

In 2022 there are two dedicated Noti showrooms, but the brand's furniture is available in other showrooms in the country. Most of the goods produced are being exported to the EU market, which is larger and more ready to pay a higher price for quality goods. The company hires about 150 employees and remains faithful to its original mission – design first, giving a special credit to the leading designers from Poland.

Balcerkiewicz has stepped down from all the executive functions while maintaining the seat of the chairman of the supervisory board in all of his ventures. The whole group: Balma, Noti and Noti showroom remain in the hands of the founder's children and his children-in-law. The succession process seems to have been successful in every case, which is not that common among family businesses. Interestingly, the Balcerkiewicz clan have been selected for the best strategist award at the Design Alive gala, and it was the first case ever that this prize was awarded to a family.[21]

5.4 Tylko

Tylko is different from every other furniture company in Poland in almost every aspect. In terms of a mindset and business model, Tylko resembles a tech company rather than a typical furniture producer. In 2021, after three rounds of financing, Tylko became one of the most valuable Polish startups.

The firm operates through e-commerce only. It does not own a single physical store, and its products can't be seen in popular showrooms. The company offers an innovative way of shopping for furniture. The typical process of diligent searching, visiting showrooms and comparing offers is replaced by a smooth digital experience full of fun and creativity.[22]

A client visiting the meticulously designed company page can choose from a limited range of storage furniture. As for February 2022, Tylko offer included bookcases, sideboards, wardrobes, TV stands, chests of drawers and shoe racks.[23] Once a piece is chosen, it can be adjusted by the client to their specific needs and tastes with the help of a friendly interactive configurator. For example, a user may change the number of rows or columns of shelving units, the color and density of the wood and the depth and height of the piece. The real treat is the Tylko app. Thanks to Augmented Reality technology, one can tailor shelves and wardrobes while watching them projected into the space they will eventually occupy. If the customer wants to experience the real colors and finishing before making their decision, there is a variety of sample kits that can be ordered on the company's page and delivered to the client's home.

Once the purchase is complete, the order is turned into a production program file and sent directly to the factory machines. After three to six weeks, the flat-packed piece arrives together with the customized, individually generated assembly manual. The assembly process is easy thanks to the unique system of patented, color-coded connectors which can be simply clicked together. Still, if the customer does not wish to engage in putting the furniture together, an optional assembly service is available in numerous European countries. When

---

[21] www.designalive.pl/balcerkiewiczowie-rodzina-ktora-postawila-na-design/ visited on February 23, 2022.

[22] https://albrechtpartners.com/mikolaj-molenda-tylko/ visited on January 21, 2022.

[23] https://tylko.com/ visited on February 11, 2022.

the piece is ready, Tylko provides a 100-day free return policy, should the customer not be entirely happy. The return shipping is free of charge within the EU. No wonders that the customer rating for the Tylko services is skyrocketing.

The key to the Tylko phenomenon is design. Everything about Tylko is purposefully designed – from the product itself to the purchasing process. The furniture has been created as an algorithm, a parametric model.[24] No matter what alterations a customer chooses, the piece will keep its aesthetic and practical value and it will be possible to produce and assembly. In other words, the playful process of configuring the furniture is "safe" for the customer, because the output will always have qualities one expects from the designer's hand – it will be artsy and ergonomic. Perhaps this unique experience of co-creating something unique without taking the risk of failure is the key to Tylko's success on the market.

The dominant business model of the furniture industry in Poland has the core activity as the production of the piece. Tylko is much more than a furniture producer, however. In fact, the production itself is outsourced to trustworthy partners in Poland – companies operating in accordance with the traditional Polish business model. Since every piece of Tylko furniture is created on demand, there is no need for giant warehouses and waste is kept at a minimum. The company operates in accordance with lean philosophy.[25] The typical struggle of a furniture company to squeeze more margins out of the chain by gaining more control of the branding or distribution process does not apply to Tylko. They play a different game. Tylko takes it all: the company controls and designs every link of the value chain and every step of the customer journey.

The Tylko brand was created in 2014 by five people: architect Mikołaj Molenda, two designers – Hanna Kokczyńska and Jacek Majewski, entrepreneur Benjamin Kuna and parametric design specialist Michał Piasecki. The latter left the firm in 2016; the remaining four formed a versatile and harmonious executive team that has led Tylko ever since.[26]

At the beginning of its journey, in 2014, Tylko took part in the pitch-competition at the prestigious San Francisco–based startup festival. The company won the Best Technical Achievement prize and made lots of new contacts, including collaboration with the prominent designer Yves Behar.[27] Soon Tylko raised $1.6 million from investors and launched their company in London in

---

[24] https://albrechtpartners.com/mikolaj-molenda-tylko/ visited on January 21, 2022.

[25] https://albrechtpartners.com/mikolaj-molenda-tylko/ visited on January 21, 2022.

[26] www.designalive.pl/tylko-historia-sukcesu-meblowych-rewolucjonistow/ visited on February 18, 2022.

[27] https://journal.tylko.com/yves-behar-customization-design/ visited on February 7, 2022.

2015. In 2016 the company raised another 3 million Euro and \$3.9 million more in 2018. In March 2021, in the middle of the worldwide COVID-19 pandemic, Tylko announced to have raised 22 million Euro in Series C.[28]

From the beginning the main market for Tylko was Western Europe – Germany, France, Great Britain and Switzerland. The company already has clients from different continents, but their real expansion is yet to come.

The year 2020 was the first year for Tylko to bring profit and income grew from EUR 16 to 36 million.[29] Yet their top priority now is not so much the profit, but rather growth. Tylko wants to become the global leader of the emerging market of the new furniture shopping: digital, user-friendly, high-quality, eco-friendly. On their Facebook page the company quotes Rami Kalish from Pitango, one of their main investors: "Tylko has a huge vision to disrupt the furniture industry that has 'frozen in time' with its outstanding technology and unwavering commitment to protect Mother Earth."[30]

In 2020 Custom Ltd. (the company that owns the Tylko brand) recorded a 128% increase in net income, winning sixty-seventh place on the list of the largest furniture producers in Poland. The net income for 2020 was approximately EUR 28 million (Wydawnictwo Meble.pl, 2022).

5.5 Deftrans

Deftrans is a company that understood and exploited a particular niche, namely, bathroom furniture production. The distinct production process as well as distribution channels makes bathroom furniture production different and requires a different strategic approach.

5.5.1 History

The history of the company began when Tomasz Defratyka, a part-time law student from western Poland, got a job at Pelipal, a small subsidiary of the German producer of bathroom furniture. The job was demanding; the future entrepreneur had a chance to get to know almost every important aspect of the trade. That's why within about three years Defratyka was ready to start his own business – importing bathroom furniture from Spain. In 1996 Deftrans company came into being. Import soon became less profitable, however, so Tomasz, with some help from his brother, decided to start up production (Hryniewicki, 2018).

---

[28] www.ft.com/content/cc15e48e-3453-11e5-bdbb-35e55cbae175?fbclid=IwAR1qfPlMc EXzhFP3EaCZIlw2HoEGT_9w-KZiYd6dmnrTUrogzey96-uHj4M#axzz3hBmUQZ2f visited on February 23, 2022.

[29] www.designalive.pl/tylko-historia-sukcesu-meblowych-rewolucjonistow/ visited on February 23, 2022.

[30] www.facebook.com/tylko/ post from March 21, 2021.

The region was rich in furniture industry specialists, so the young entrepreneur did not have a problem with building a professional factory despite his lack of experience in carpentry. The first production hall was very primitive and – just as in the case of Nowy Styl some years earlier – it happened to be a former fertilizer warehouse. The business flourished and within a couple of years Deftrans products were available in the whole country.

In the early 2000s Deftrans started exporting its products to Hungary and the Netherlands thanks to contacts from the Poznan fair. Interestingly enough, Deftrans was hardly present on the German market, which is the key market for the majority of Polish furniture exporters. The company believed the German market to be "too difficult" and never made a substantial effort to get a piece of the German cake.

In early 2006 Deftrans opened a new, modern production facility of 4,000 m² in Odolany. The business-friendly approach of the local authorities was critical (Hryniewicki, 2018).

In the second decade of the twenty-first century Deftrans entered the sector of kitchen furniture creating a new brand – Fig. The production technology is the same as in the case of bathroom furniture. When it comes to the economy sector, the distribution channels are also similar, namely, DIY and home improvement retailers.

Deftrans is a family firm – with Tomasz as the chairman and his wife Edyta as the deputy-chairman of the board. They are both involved in community outreach, having founded two educational institutions for the local children – the Astrid Lindgren School and a multipurpose center for education and leisure.

In 2022 Deftrans owns three brands: Nefra for the middle and upper-middle sectors of bathroom furniture, NAS for economy sector of bathroom furniture and Fig – the brand for the economy sector of kitchen furniture. The company closed the year 2021 with a revenue of approximately EUR 33 million, yet the owner stated that with rising costs, profitability dropped despite higher revenues.[31]

5.5.2 Particularities of the Sector

The important factor shaping the marketing of bathroom furnishing is its close dependence on the sanitary ware. It is the choice of the sink that determines the choice of the furniture. The big sanitary ware producers usually provide the no-name shelves that accompany their sinks. The set is sold under the brand name of the sanitary ware producers (Hryniewicki, 2018). The furniture producers use the reverse approach – they treat sink as a commodity and sell the sink and

---

[31] https://biznes.meble.pl/biznes-room,przychody-rosna-ale-wynika-to-ze-wzrostu-cen,796.html.

furniture set under their own brand name. For a client, the product is always the same set, but the two industries are rivals for value capture. The convergence between the industry of bathroom furniture and sanitary ware is even stronger due to the same distribution channels: large home improvement retailers for the economy segment and bathroom salons for the middle and upper segment.

The brand name recognition for bathroom furniture companies is very low among end users, whereas they do recognize some sanitary ware brands. The furniture producers, therefore, try to make their brands better known not only to the retailers, but also to the individual clients.

The higher-value segments of the market differ from the lower ones in two important aspects. The first one is obviously the quality – design, ergonomics as well as the quality of varnish, hinges and fittings. The second factor is connected with the logistics: the economy segment furniture is transported in pieces and assembled on the spot, whereas higher-class bathroom furniture must be assembled by the manufacturer and transported in a ready-to-use state.

The recognition and exploitation of all these particularities made Deftrans one of the key players on the domestic market of bathroom furniture (even though approximately half of the production volume is being exported) (Hryniewicki, 2018).

The COVID pandemic period was used for the rebranding process (e.g. a new, more user-friendly site) and modernization of the production lines. Yet in early 2022 Tomasz Defratyka declared that the rise in production costs caused a sudden drop in profitability.[32]

5.6 Miloni

Miloni is a small company and a niche brand built around the main type of products: high-quality solid-wood tables. Miloni is the example of "craft 2.0" – a mixture of traditional carpentry and modern design and marketing. It is established by and targeted at the generation that can hardly remember the communist times, but has appreciation for timeless beauty, ecology and slow living.

5.6.1 The History

Mateusz Nowotnik, the owner and co-founder of Miloni, replicated the history of many leading Polish furniture producers in one important aspect: he was the son of a carpenter. Mateusz, like many of today's CEOs, associates his childhood with the smell of wood from his father's workshop. His passion for solid

---

[32] https://biznes.meble.pl/biznes-room,przychody-rosna-ale-wynika-to-ze-wzrostu-cen,796.html.

wood is not just a slogan – one can see it in every interview and, more importantly, in every product.

The youth of Mateusz Nowotnik, however, took place in the 2000s, so he did not have a chance to catch the bandwagon of the export boom in the 1990s, when most of his older colleagues built their fortunes. Mateusz, a mechanical engineer by profession, simply got a job in the wood industry: first in maintenance and later as production supervisor or manager of the technology and development department.[33]

Having the inherited passion for wood and the experience with timber industry, Mateusz decided to start his own company. Again, like in many other Polish cases, it was a family business. Mateusz joined forces with his brother-in-law Przemysław Fornal, an industrial designer and furniture technician, and they set up a company specializing in simple, beautiful, high-quality tables. It was indeed a refreshing idea in 2012 when they started.[34]

Soon Przemek decided that as much as he loved design, he wasn't much into developing production, buying carpentry machines or hiring people, so he left the company and it has been run by Mateusz ever since. Mateusz is overlooking the business side, while Magda Nowotnik, his wife and an architect by profession, takes care of the entire marketing – brand building, social media and the like. Mateusz' father also joined the family endeavor and – as a professional carpenter – he oversees the production process.[35]

5.6.2 The Business Model

The company controls the entire process of production – from designing the piece, purchasing a log in the forest, through cutting, seasoning, drying, pretreatment, to the finished piece of furniture and shipment. The tables are produced on demand, and the company also takes special orders for highly customized pieces. Additionally, the company has introduced an innovating method of stabilizing the wood through three-layer gluing. This innovation makes it possible to produce folded tables resistant to temperature and humidity changes.

The signature products of Miloni are "tables for life" as the brand slogan proclaims.[36] All the pieces are carefully designed to emphasize the natural beauty of the solid oak wood they are made of. Other products (chests of drawers, desks

---

[33] https://biznes.meble.pl/biznes-room,czujemy-sie-rzemieslnikami-2-0,793.html.

[34] https://biznes.meble.pl/biznes-room,czujemy-sie-rzemieslnikami-2-0,793.html visited on February 27, 2022.

[35] https://biznes.meble.pl/biznes-room,czujemy-sie-rzemieslnikami-2-0,793.html visited on February 27, 2022.

[36] https://magazif.com/ludzie/niewielka-manufaktura-i-wielkie-rzemioslo/?fbclid=IwAR2uOa Pu8ERcRcXjoffhC6jQJfP0JsHtlUduKRxrcpq8itbAt3-Xobv3VZQ visited on February 24, 2022.

and sometimes chairs) are intended to complement the tables and never over-shadow them. The pieces are expensive, targeted at upper-middle class sensitive to design, ecology and responsible development. The products are distributed through e-commerce (the brand e-shop) and various partner showrooms in the country. Most of the table models were designed by Przemysław Fornal (the co-founder of the firm) or Magda Nowotnik, but recently Miloni began cooperation with one of the most prominent Polish designers – Tomek Rygalik.[37]

5.6.3 The Brand

The important part of the Miloni brand identity is its connection with the traditional craft. Although Miloni's products are made with the help of sophis-ticated machinery, the production requires a much human engagement, skill, artistry and precision. The firm also preserves the spirit of carpentry craftsman-ship. As a member of a guild, Miloni educates future carpenters as interns. The young people from a nearby vocational school have the unique chance to not only deal with the actual manufacturing process, but to observe the entire value chain of furniture production.[38]

Recently, five Polish furniture brands drawing from traditional craft joined forces and created a common project "Kolektywni" (Collective) to promote their design and philosophy. The collective is very active on social media and other PR activities.[39]

5.6.4 Challenges

The quality and beauty of the furniture that Miloni produces depends largely on the availability of high-quality oak wood. Mateusz complains that the most beautiful pieces of oak wood that have been grown on the local soil for 200 years are sold on open bidding auctions available to everyone. The young Polish companies usually cannot outbid the old Italian giants buying the large amount of the most valuable timber from the State Forest agency. Mateusz believes such a practice to be short-sighted and unfair toward the local craftsmen.

5.7 RC Design

RC Design is an example of the effective exploitation of the traditional, production-focused subcontracting business model. The company is moderate

---

[37] https://biznes.meble.pl/biznes-room,czujemy-sie-rzemieslnikami-2-0,793.html visited on February 27, 2022.

[38] www.youtube.com/watch?v=rpE1_H3YJjc visited on May 4, 2022.

[39] www.dobrzemieszkaj.pl/galeria/polscy_designerzy_lacza_sily_grupa_kolektywni_zrzesza_marki_meblarskie,308037-763276.html visited on March 1, 2022.

in size – it hires about sixty people and has two production sites in central Poland. RC Design specializes in the small-batch production of luxurious furniture, especially those of unusual shape or structure. The firm has established its position and enjoys an impeccable opinion within its proper niche. Thus, it gets contracts that require precision and trustworthiness, but often bring in higher (two-digit) margins than generic projects. In addition to the core business (producing furniture as subcontractor), the owner of the company seeks other business model options, such as their own premium brand of furniture and production of innovative ecological materials.

The story and business model of RC Design is closely linked with the biography of its founder, Rafał Cebula. His passion for furniture started early – as a five-year-old, he would play with the shavings and watch his father – a carpentry master – at work. Despite the family's objections, young Rafał pursued the education path of carpentry and wood technology. He did not abandon his passion for beautiful furniture even when he took jobs in other sectors. This period gave him a lot of contacts and business know-how that he eventually exploited once he decided to return to his original dream and start furniture production. And so in 2006 Rafał Cebula co-created the WRS Design company that would eventually (after the partnership split) lead to the foundation of RC Design. Cebula's DNA is all over the place. Not only is the company named after its founder but, more importantly, it clearly is the vehicle to pursue his unique dreams and interests. As for 2022, there are three of them: luxury furniture production, Go.Ce – a signature collection of premium furniture – and research into new, more ecological materials for furniture production.[40]

The WRS Design firm managed to gain the first contracts for luxury goods thanks to the contacts of the founders. As soon as the production was completed flawlessly, the word spread and the next contacts came from recommendations. One of the most prominent projects the firm realized was the production of furniture for the entire network of Michael Kors boutiques in Europe. WRS Design (RC Design after the split and rebranding of the company) has carried out numerous projects for luxury brands. The list of clients is long and includes jewelry and watches stores (Lalique, Hublot, Jaeger-Lecoultre), fashion boutiques (Valentino, Maxmara, Pinko), beauty products retailers, hotels and restaurants (Sheraton, Mariott, IBIS) as well as prestigious public spaces (NATO conference facility in Warsaw, concert halls, churches, etc.).[41]

The type of business model that RC Design accepts has its advantages and disadvantages. As it was noted before, the final client for premium goods is not

---

[40] www.youtube.com/watch?v=Lfnn4dRWmiA visited on March 15, 2022.
[41] www.rcdesign.pl/realizacje/.

very price-sensitive, so there is space for slightly higher margins. 10% net margin is believed to be "decent," yet not always achievable. Moreover, the market is limited; once the firm gains the trust of the main contractor, usually a design studio, they have the chance to remain on the market and be recommended further. Last not least, there is a magic to luxury furniture – the elegance and beauty of the goods produced may help you attract people who would not work just anywhere.

However, there are also challenges. In order to be able to produce complicated, unique pieces, the firm needs to have top-quality machines and the staff must be trained for years and later – kept happy. This means that costs are stable, so the firm needs to maintain a stable level of income. This means they constantly need to close new deals and bring in new clients to keep the costly employees and machines busy. This isn't always easy. The 2020 pandemic was particularly challenging. RC Design has had very few private clients – they usually work business to business. When the pandemic hit the HoReCa sector and shopping malls, the prospects for the firm were rather dim. The public anti-COVID support system helped the firm to survive the difficulties.

Another challenge is linked to human capital. Every producer in the industry is struggling now, as there are not enough skilled people on the labor market. Yet when producing high-quality products, some of the employees are almost irreplaceable, which creates a lot of pressure in terms of proper human capital management.

The third challenge is sometimes a complicated communication channel with the end-client. There are many practical issues that the designers overlook, and they need to be solved quickly at the level pf production or assembly. If there is a pyramid of middlemen between the furniture producer and the final client, the effect might be unsatisfactory, and the reputation of the firm stained with no fault of their own.

All these challenges may bring a serious threat to the profitability and even existence of the firm, as the COVID-19 pandemic period has proven. Be it for this reason or due to Rafał Cebula's personal aspirations, RC Design has been exploring other areas and business models. The first one is their very own signature furniture line, designed in collaboration with the design studio of the architect Hernan Gomez under the common brand name Go.Ce. The two gentlemen designed and created prototypes for a whole line of luxury furniture inspired by yachts, plant shapes and melodies. In 2019 the catalogues and prototypes were ready and the marketing and PR campaign began. And then the pandemic hit before there was a single client interested in the new brand. Eventually the prototypes were sold to a showroom in Dubai, and the further fate of the collection is yet to be known.

Another path that the company has been exploring is that of ecological materials. Rafał Cebula took a great interest in Oxytrees (the type of tree that grows very fast and absorbs a lot of CO_2 while growing) and plywood made of annual plants such as hemp, goldenrod or miscanthus. The company – in association with other institutions – is conducting research on the large-scale applications of such materials, at this stage without a clear vision of commercialization.[42]

6 Conclusions

This Element has made an attempt to immerse the reader in the living world of the strategists of the Polish furniture industry. It has been our aim to give as broad as possible account the range of phenomena that together shape the industry, including some rarely included in strategy books. As tour guides, we wished to lead the reader not only to the most famous or most important places, but also to the ones located off the beaten track, but nevertheless having beauty and importance. In conclusion, let's emphasize the most important elements of the whole story.

The country of Poland has been a favorable place for furniture production due to its location and richness of timber. Yet the history of the nation, or more precisely, its long-lasting political dependence on neighboring empires, has prevented the formation of a strong infrastructure or institutions. Until 1989, no business endeavor had a chance to last and develop without experiencing turbulence, exploitation or marginalization by the ruling powers. Perhaps the years of constant challenges, scarcity and discontinuity have allowed Polish craftsmen to develop the skill of bricolage, the art of making lemonade out of the lemons at hand. This skill came in handy when the short window of great opportunity opened in 1989 – a period of enormous demand in the East, economic and political freedom coupled with capital, raw material and technology shortages, lack of management know-how and unstable legal and fiscal systems.

Within just over three decades since the fall of communism, the Polish furniture industry as we know it has emerged. Today, it is marked by the past in various ways. The majority of companies remain in the hands of families, with all the ensuing consequences: a strong culture, long-lasting strategies, the reluctance to mergers and the constant temptation to micromanage. The industry remains scattered and suspicious with respect to radical innovations. At the same time, it is dynamic, self-aware and extremely resilient.

---

[42] www.rp.pl/biznes/art8798931-ekskluzywne-polskie-meble-z-topinamburu visited on March 15, 2022.

Impressive production capacities and skills have become the hallmark of Poland and the core of the business models – for better or for worse. The industry consists mostly of exquisite furniture makers, but it has only a few brilliant strategists who are able to lead their businesses into the league of international champions.

The once peripheral and colonial status of Poland is now reflected in the subordinate role of Polish producers in value chains and, thus, in the value capture game. A pay gap has developed for historical reasons, one which is hard to close with individual efforts. Thus, the industry is looking for a boost to push the entire branch up to a higher gear. Some hopes had been placed in the activity of the Polish government, but the industry seems rather disappointed with the outcome of these efforts. The other hope of the industry is to jump on the bandwagon of the forthcoming revolution and let it shift the division of power to their advantage. That is why the concepts of Industry 4.0 and e-commerce have gained interest among Polish furniture producers.

The mosaic of so many (32,000!) companies includes many different business models mirroring the aspirations, talent and life goals of their respective entrepreneurs. The seven case studies in Section 5 offer examples of life stories unfolding in particular contexts and intertwined with the creation of unique firms, each of them successful on their own terms. What these cases have in common is the courage, stamina and vivid imagination of the entrepreneurs themselves, who have managed to turn the uncertainty and chaos around them into prolific, logical and profit-making businesses. At the end of the day, this Element is a commentary to the achievements of these entrepreneurs and their likes.

References

Books

Single Author, Single Volume

Gaweł, Ł. (2007). *Stanisław Wyspiański: Życie i twórczość.* Wydawnictwo Kluszczyński.

Hryniewicki, M. (2015). *Biznesmeni i wizjonerzy.* Wydawnictwo meble.pl.

Hryniewicki, T. (2018). *Wizjonerzy i biznesmeni, część II.* Wydawnictwo meble.pl.

Kalupa, Ł. (2004). *Meblarstwo w Polsce: Kondycja, podstawy sukcesu, perspektywy.* Wydawnictwo Eint.

Knight, F. H. (1921). *Risk, Uncertainty and Profit.* Houghton Mifflin Company.

Kostrzyńska-Miłosz, A. (2005). *Polskie meble 1918–1939: Forma, funkcja, technika.* Instytut Sztuki Polskiej Akademii Nauk.

Kostrzyńska-Miłosz, A. (2019). *Stylistic Trends in Polish Furniture 1918-1939.* Instytut Sztuki PAN.

Kula, W. (1947). *Historia gospodarcza polski, w dobie popowstaniowej, 1864–1918.* Spółdzielnia Wydawnicza "Wiedza."

Latusek-Jurczak, D. (2017). *Zarządzanie w Polsce. Dydaktyczne studia przypadków.* Poltext.

Maszkowska, B. (1956). *Z dziejów polskiego meblarstwa okresu Oświecenia.* Zakład Imienia Ossolińskich – Wydawnictwo.

Pachelska, H. (2003). *Przemiany techniczne i technologiczne w przemyśle drzewnym na ziemiach polskich w latach 1870–1939.* Wydawn. SGGW.

Penrose, E. (1959). *The Theory of the Growth of the Firm.* John Wiley & Sons.

Spender, J. C. (2014). *Business Strategy: Managing Uncertainty, Opportunity, and Enterprise.* Oxford University Press.

Żeleński, T. (1973). *O Wyspiańskim.* Wydawnictwo Literackie.

Joint Authors, Single Volume

Jezierski, A., & Leszczynska, C. (1997). *Historia gospodarcza Polski.* Key Text.

Journal Articles

Bowman, C., & Ambrosini, V. (2000). Value Creation versus Value Capture: Towards a Coherent Definition of Value in Strategy. *British Journal of Management, 11*(1), 1–15. https://doi.org/10.1111/1467-8551.00147.

Flyvbjerg, B. (2006). Five Misunderstandings about Case-Study Research. *Qualitative Inquiry, 12*(2), 219–245. https://doi.org/10.1177/1077800405 284363.

Gans, J., & Ryall, M. D. (2017). Value Capture Theory: A Strategic Management Review. *Strategic Management Journal, 38*(1), 17–41. https://doi.org/10.1002/smj.2592.

Gereffi, G., Humphrey, J., & Sturgeon, T. (2005). The Governance of Global Value Chains. *Review of International Political Economy, 12*, 78–104. https://doi.org/10.1080/09692290500049805.

Gibbon, P., Bair, J., & Ponte, S. (2008). Governing Global Value Chains. *Economy and Society – ECON SOC, 37*, 315–338. https://doi.org/10.1080/03085140802172656.

Hoffmannová, J. (1989). Chancellor Metternich and Inventor Michael Thonet. *East Central Europe, 16*(1–2), 135–143. https://doi.org/10.1163/1876330 89X00087.

Humphrey, J., & Schmitz, H. (2002). How Does Insertion in Global Value Chains Affect Upgrading in Industrial Clusters? *Regional Studies, 36*(9), 1017–1027.

Ingold, T. (2017). Anthropology Contra Ethnography. *Hau: Journal of Ethnographic Theory, 7*(1), 21–26. https://doi.org/10.14318/hau7.1.005.

Kyriazidou, E., & Pesendorfer, M. (1999). Viennese Chairs: A Case Study for Modern Industrialization. *The Journal of Economic History, 59*(1), 143–166. https://doi.org/10.1017/S0022050700022324.

Pachelska, H. (2007). International Trade in Timber and Wood Products in Poland between WW1 and WW2. *Intercathedra, 23*, 102–107.

Powell, T. C. (2014). Strategic Management and the Person. *Strategic Organization, 12*(3), 200–207. https://doi.org/10.1177/1476127014544093.

Sarasvathy, S. D. (2001). Causation and Effectuation: Toward a Theoretical Shift from Economic Inevitability to Entrepreneurial Contingency. *Academy of Management Review, 26*(2), 243–263. https://doi.org/10.5465/amr.2001.4378020.

Whittington, R. (1996). Strategy as practice. *Long Range Planning, 29*(5), 731–735. https://doi.org/10.1016/0024-6301(96)00068-4.

Technical Reports

B+R STUDIO Tomasz Wiktorski. (2022). *Polskie meble. Outlook. Raport 2022.* https://brstudio.eu/.

Meblarski 1000. Zestawienie największych producentów mebli w Polsce. Edycja 2021. (2022) Wydawnictwo Meble.pl https://biznes.meble.pl/aktual nosci,meblarski-1000-ranking-najwiekszych,17475.html.

Inter IKEA Systems B. V. (2021). *IKEA: Made in Poland.* www.ikea.com/pl/pl/ files/pdf/f5/9e/f59ea314/ikea-raport-made-in-poland-2021-eng-web.pdf.

Ministerstwo Rozwoju. (2017). *Strategia na Rzecz Odpowiedzialnego Rozwoju do 2020 (z perspektywą do 2030).* www.gov.pl/web/fundusze-regiony/strate gia-na-rzecz-odpowiedzialnego-rozwoju.

OIGPM (Ogólnopolska Izba Gospodarcza Producentów Mebli). (2022). *Poland: Smart Furniture Export Catalogue.* https://issuu.com/oigpm/docs/ catalog2021_web.

PARP (Polska Agencja Rozwoju Przedsiębiorczości). (2018a). *Analiza obecnych zasobów, potencjału i międzynarodowej pozycji konkurencyjnej polskiej branży meblarskiej.* www.parp.gov.pl/component/site/site/strategia-marki-branzy-meblarskiej.

PARP (Polska Agencja Rozwoju Przedsiębiorczości). (2018b). *Analiza potrzeb i oczekiwań w zakresie wspólnej marki polskiej branży meblarskiej.* www.parp.gov.pl/component/site/site/strategia-marki-branzy-meblarskiej.

Pekao SA. (2021). *Polskie meblarstwo 4.0 Jak przebiega ewolucja krajowego sektora w stronę nowych motorów wzrostu?* https://media.pekao.com.pl/pr/ 693977/raport-banku-pekao-sytuacja-i-wyzwania-branzy-meblarskiej-w-polsce.

PFR (Polski Fundusz Rozwoju). (2021). *Kompendium polskie meble.* https://pfr.pl/ dam/jcr:aa553360-d536-4f65-a9e9-04a00ed3a1b5/PFR_meble_202107.pdf.

PKO BP. (2021). *Branża Meblarska: Pozycja Międzynarodowa Polskich Producentów W Obliczu Kryzysu Wywołanego Przez Pandemię Covid-19.* www.pkobp.pl/media_files/8af78743-0691-49ff-acb7-305a70978ef7.pdf.

Acknowledgments

First of all, I would like to thank JC Spender. His view on strategy took me on a decade-long intellectual journey and prompted to write this Element.

I want to express my gratitude to my family. My children: Jadwiga, Jeremi, Salomea and Miriam Łuczewscy endured my writing days with much patience and sweetness. My parents, Maria Brańka-Bednarz and Marek Bednarz, were my angels; most of this Element was written in their hospitable home while they were taking care of my four children. Last not least, my thanks go to my husband Dr. Hab. Michał Łuczewski – I don't know where to start. Thank you for your love, support and sacrifice.

The research behind this Element was conducted within a team – I want to thank Dr. Karolina Dudek, Piotr Paczyński, Dr. Anna Sabat and Dr. Sylwia Oleńska. It's been a pleasure to have worked with you.

The process of writing can be tricky, and especially in a world touched be a world pandemic or a ruthless attack on a neighboring country I needed all the encouragement and support in the world, and I received it from many wonderful people. Thank you, Dr. Elżbieta Wyrzykowska, Adam Lewkowicz, Marta Kiela-Czarnik, Magda Dzięgielewska, Krzysztof Pałys OP and the entire Tshuva community. I would also like to thank Dr. Natalia Banasik-Jemielniak, Dr. Karolina Lewestam and Rafał Świeżak.

The Polish furniture industry itself consists of so many helpful and generous people. My warmest thanks go to Dr. Tomasz Wiktorski, Marek Hryniewicki and all my interviewees.

Among my numerous talents there isn't one connected with paperwork. I would be lost without the help of Magdalena Klimaszewska and Andrzej Krzyżewski from Kozminski University.

I would like to thank the National Science Centre for the research grant that enabled me to conduct research and write this Element.

Cambridge Elements

Business Strategy

J.-C. Spender
Kozminski University
J.-C. Spender is a research Professor, Kozminski University. He has been active in the business strategy field since 1971 and is the author or co-author of 7 books and numerous papers. His principal academic interest is in knowledge-based theories of the private sector firm, and managing them.

Advisory Board
Jay Barney, *Eccles School of Business, The University of Utah*
Stewart Clegg, *University of Technology, Sydney*
Thomas Durand, *Conservatoire National des Arts et Métiers, Paris*
CT Foo, *Independent Scholar, Singapore*
Robert Grant, *Bocconi University, Milan*
Robin Holt, *Copenhagen Business School*
Paula Jarzabkowski, *Cass School, City University, London*
Naga Lakshmi Damaraju, *Indian School of Business*
Marjorie Lyles, *Kelley School of Business, Indiana University*
Joseph T. Mahoney, *College of Business, University of Illinois at Urbana-Champaign*
Nicolai Foss, *Bocconi University, Milan*
Andreas Scherer, *University of Zurich*
Deepak Somaya, *College of Business, University of Illinois at Urbana-Champaign*
Eduard van Gelderen, *Chief Investment Officer, APG, Amsterdam*

About the Series
Business strategy's reach is vast, and important too since wherever there is business activity there is strategizing. As a field, strategy has a long history from medieval and colonial times to today's developed and developing economies. This series offers a place for interesting and illuminating research including industry and corporate studies, strategizing in service industries, the arts, the public sector, and the new forms of Internet-based commerce. It also covers today's expanding gamut of analytic techniques.

Cambridge Elements ≡

Business Strategy

Elements in the Series

Knowledge Strategies
Constantin Bratianu

Dynamic Capabilities: History and an Extension
Bart Nooteboom

Blockchains
Wenqian Wang, Fabrice Lumineau and Oliver Schilke

The Creative Response: Knowledge and Innovation
Cristiano Antonelli and Alessandra Colombelli

Strategy-Making and Organizational Evolution: A Managerial Agency Perspective
Robert Alexander Burgelman, Yuliya Snihur and Llewellyn Douglas
William Thomas

Strategy-In-Practices: A Process-Philosophical Perspective on Strategy-Making
Robert C. H. Chia and David Mackay

Strategizing AI in Business and Education: Emerging Technologies and Business Strategy
Aleksandra Przegalinska and Dariusz Jemielniak

Sustainable Value Chains in the Global Garment Industry
Rachel Alexander and Peter Lund-Thomsen

Business Model Innovation: Strategic and Organizational Issues for Established Firms
Constantinos Markides

Evolution of the Automobile Industry: A Capability-Architecture-Performance Approach
Takahiro Fujimoto

People Centric Innovation Ecosystem: Japanese Management and Practices
Yingying Zhang-Zhang and Takeo Kikkawa

Strategizing in the Polish Furniture Industry
Paulina Bednarz-Łuczewska

A full series listing is available at: www.cambridge.org/EBUS

Printed in the United States
by Baker & Taylor Publisher Services